# THE SIXTIES SOUNDS THAT MADE THE NORTH EAST SWING

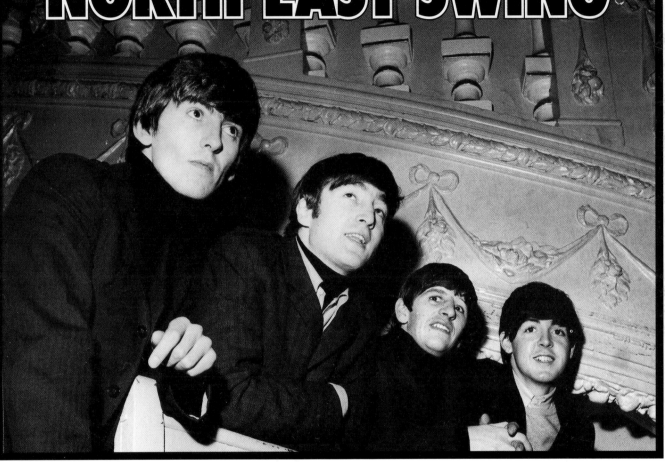

by

**Mel Kirtley**

# ACKNOWLEDGEMENTS

I would like to express my gratitude to the management and staff of Northeast Press (publishers of The Sunderland Echo, The Hartlepool Mail and The Shields Gazette) for their assistance with the publication of this book.

I wish to thank Stuart Bell, Managing Director of Northeast Press, for supporting the publication of the book and for allowing access to the company's archive material.

*Mel Kirtley*
*1997*

---

*All advertisements are reproduced courtesy of*
*The Sunderland Echo, The Hartlepool Mail and The Shields Gazette.*

*All photographs are reproduced from the collections of*
*The Sunderland Echo and The Shields Gazette.*

*All top ten charts are as originally used in The Sunderland Echo to represent record sales on Wearside.*
*The data is reproduced by kind permission of The Sunderland Echo.*

*Concert memorabilia reproduced from the David Degnan Collection.*

*Artwork and design : Tracy Robertson.*
*Cover design : Mark Dorrian of The Sunderland Echo.*

*Copies of the front cover photograph of The Beatles are available from*
*The Sunderland Echo photographic department (Tel: 0191 534 3011).*

---

Published by Wearside Books.

Copyright 1997 Wearside Books.

ISBN 0 9525380 3 2.

# INTRODUCTION

It is an undeniable fact that the sixties represented the most innovative era in popular music.

From the early years of Billy Fury, Bobby Darin, Del Shannon and Elvis Presley to the beat boom of The Beatles and The Rolling Stones and the subsequent American response of Californian sea, surf and sand courtesy of The Beach Boys, the sixties produced a creative energy which has never been eclipsed.

As the decade unfolded we were treated to the R & B sounds of the likes of Georgie Fame & The Blue Flames and The Spencer Davis Group as well as to the gentler American west coast sounds of The Byrds et al.

There was the folk-rock protest era of Bob Dylan and the almost simultaneous arrival of 'flower power' when Scott McKenzie's *San Francisco* became the anthem of 1967's Summer Of Love during which time an idealist youth culture of peace, love and psychedelia transformed much of popular music into an art form.

Just when pop music was growing too serious for its own good, Tamla Motown provided the perfect antidote with a clutch of classic dance floor hits which had been conceived with the sole intention of creating an uncomplicated feel good factor.

Looking back, the spirit of the sixties was responsible for opening a veritable Pandora's Box of musical tricks. It was that same spirit which swept all before it and in doing so created a stupendous movement which broke down more musical barriers than any previous generation had hitherto thought possible.

The music of the sixties was spontaneous by nature and generally less self indulgent than that of subsequent decades. That said, the energies expended in breaking new ground during the swinging sixties resulted in an inevitable situation of having less to discover in later years and a scenario in which much of the music from the seventies onwards has either been a derivative or a reincarnation of an earlier sixties sound.

*Flyleaf Caption*
*THE BEATLES appeared at Empire Theatre, Sunderland twice during 1963 and were captured on camera at the theatre by a Sunderland Echo photographer.*

---

**Artistes featured in the biographical sections were chosen in an attempt to cover as wide a range of popular music as possible. While similar volumes of space have been given to the potted biographies of each act, this does not indicate a naive belief by the author that, for example, The Beatles and Brian Hyland made equal contributions to the music scene of the sixties.**

**Records chosen for inclusion in The Ones That Got Away section reflect the author's personal choice.**

**The quiz at the rear of the book is intended purely as light hearted fun with no prizes other than the self satisfaction of achieving a high score.**

# THE SWINGING SIXTIES

Contrary to popular myth, the sixties did not begin to swing at the start of the new decade. Pop music during the first year of the sixties was merely an extension of the late fifties and there was little audible sign of the progression to what is generally regarded as the sounds of the swinging sixties.

The first Wearside chart of 1960, as published in the Sunderland Echo, featured names of such fifties stalwarts as Russ Conway, Anthony Newley, Michael Holliday, Tommy Steele and Guy Mitchell.

The music of the time was American influenced with the likes of Elvis Presley, Neil Sedaka, Bobby Darin, Connie Francis and Duane Eddy dominating the listings. There were of course several home grown stars although many of them played music which bore more than a passing resemblance to that of their Stateside cousins. Adam Faith's first three chart hits, *What Do You Want, Poor Me* and *Someone Else's Baby,* cloned the music of Buddy Holly while Billy Fury's earliest efforts drew comparisons with those of Elvis Presley.

Skiffle was still a force to be reckoned with and Lonnie Donegan enjoyed a most productive year with *My Old Man's A Dustman, I Wanna Go Home* and *Lorelei*. The charts were nothing if not varied. Perry Como, Max Bygraves and Charlie Drake mixed it with Gene Vincent and Marty Wilde, while twenty year old Neil Sedaka became an early pioneer of the singer-songwriter scene.

Cliff Richard and Elvis Presley continued to rule the roost, Roy Orbison made his chart debut with *Only The Lonely* and one of the first so-called 'death discs' to make it in Britain climbed all the way to number one. The song was *Tell Laura I Love Her* and the singer, Ricky Valance, was one of the earliest one-hit-wonders to top the charts before slipping into subsequent chart obscurity.

The charts of 1960 were strong on instrumentals. As well as the hits of The Shadows and Duane Eddy, the year produced notable successes for Acker Bilk, John Barry Seven, The Ventures and Johnny & The Hurricanes.

Johnny Kidd & The Pirates recorded *Shakin' All Over* which many people to this day regard as a milestone in British Rock & Roll music, while one leading music paper described Rolf Harris' Wobble Board invention as the 'new sound of a new decade'. The record which caused all the excitement was *Tie Me Kangaroo Down Sport*.

With the general lack of a definite music trend, records succeeded or failed on their own merits as perceived by the record buying public rather than because of their proximity to the latest fashionable sound niche. However that was soon to change and 1960 was to be the swansong for many hitherto chart artistes. The Platters, Frankie Laine, Michael Holliday, Fats Domino and Tommy Steele are just some of the names for whom the going got tough from 1961 onwards and many would never chart in a major way again.

By 1961, alarm bells began ringing in Rock & Roll circles as the two principle U.K. chart purveyors of the music showed signs of moving away from their roots and began to gradually soften their approach. The transition was particularly successful for Elvis Presley who subsequently experienced his best chart year to date with four chart toppers, of which *Are You Lonesome Tonight, Wooden Heart* and *Surrender* all exposed the gentler side of his music. Meanwhile, our top home grown exponent of Rock & Roll, Billy Fury, aimed his post 1960 record releases firmly towards the mainstream pop market. *Halfway To Paradise, I'd Never Find Another You* and a revival of *Jealousy* all signified a departure from Fury's recognised former territory although on stage he maintained a strong Rock & Roll presence.

1961 saw the launch of Helen Shapiro's recording career as the mature voiced fourteen year old was propelled to stardom on the back of her debut single *Don't Treat Me Like A Child* and her two subsequent chart toppers *You Don't Know* and *Walkin' Back To Happiness*.

American record label Tamla Records clocked-up its first Stateside million seller with The Miracles' *Shop Around* which hardly created a stir in this country other than to whet the appetite for what was to come three years down the line. By the end of the year, Tamla chief Berry Gordy launched his second record label in America, Motown Records, little knowing that the eventual fusion of the two labels would unleash one of the most potent forces on to the recording industry.

The end of 1961 saw the arrival of The Twist as the latest worldwide dance craze although the first signs of major British record sales associated with the dance had to wait until the following year, courtesy of Chubby Checker.

The first chart of 1962 saw *Moon River* by Danny Williams in pole position before being replaced in mid January by one of the year's longest running chart toppers; *The Young Ones* by Cliff Richard & The Shadows.

The year was notable for longevity at number one with just twelve chart toppers throughout 1962. An insight into the year's musical tastes may be gleaned from the nature of the material which hit top spot and the length of time which it spent there. Longest running number ones included *The Young Ones* by Cliff Richard & The Shadows (6 weeks), *Wonderful Land* by The Shadows (8 weeks), *Good Luck Charm* by Elvis Presley (5 weeks), *I Remember You* by Frank Ifield (7 weeks), *Telstar* by The Tornados (5 weeks) and *Lovesick Blues* by Frank Ifield (5 weeks).

The advent of the actor-singer scaled new heights when Richard Chamberlain (aka Dr. Kildare) hit the charts twice while the ascendancy of one of the year's most unusual releases, *Nut Rocker* by B. Bumble & The Stingers, to the chart summit raised one or two eyebrows in the classical music fraternity.

1962 was probably the last year in which comedy records stood a healthy chance of reaching the charts with both Mike Sarne (*Come Outside* and *Will I What*) and Bernard Cribbins (*Hole In The Ground* and *Right Said Fred*) becoming unlikely pop stars. The two Bernard Cribbins hits were produced by George Martin shortly before he became a leading light in the recording career of The Beatles.

While both Britain and America somewhat complacently considered that they had successfully transcended the, by now, passé Rock & Roll phenomenon, a clutch of young musicians were perfecting their trade in the Hamburg clubs. The embryonic stars of tomorrow who took up short term residency in West Germany included The Beatles, Gerry & The Pacemakers and The Searchers. The face of popular music was soon to change forever ......

1963 started in unspectacular fashion. Indeed, for the first quarter of the year it was a case of as-you-were with Cliff Richard, Frank Ifield and The Shadows continuing to dominate the top of the charts. Towards the end of the previous year The Beatles had released their debut single *Love Me Do* which just scraped into the lower reaches of the top twenty while Bob Dylan's first LP unceremoniously hit the record shops. Neither piece of vinyl caused any noticeable excitement.

By April, Merseybeat had arrived and Liverpool acts had virtually taken over the charts and the music scene in general. The Beatles, Gerry & The Pacemakers, The Searchers and Billy J. Kramer & The Dakotas virtually killed off all competition for top spot in the U.K. singles charts and in doing so they stood the record industry on its head. Such was the dominance of beat groups and the stranglehold which they had on the charts that from 11th April until the end of the year they occupied the coveted number one spot for all but three weeks.

By the end of the year the beat group phenomenon included groups from not only Liverpool but also from towns and cities throughout the U.K. Dagenham's Brian Poole & The Tremeloes (whose acceptance by Decca Records at the expense of The Beatles is one of the best documented events in the entire history of pop music) hit top spot with *Do You Love Me* while Tottenham's Dave Clark Five were already flexing their muscles for an assault on the new year's chart. There were also early career hits from Freddie & The Dreamers and The Hollies (both from Manchester) as well as The Fourmost and The Merseybeats (Liverpool) and Manfred Mann (London).

The first new number one of 1964 was The Dave Clark Fives' *Glad All Over* which, having displaced The Beatles' *I Want To Hold Your Hand,* immediately set the tabloid press screaming such headlines as "Tottenham's Answer To The Beatles". The accolade was to be somewhat exaggerated in this country but the act did take America by storm and helped to establish Britain as the worldwide nerve centre of the recording industry. British beat groups had become a global institution.

By mid 1964, The Rolling Stones' chart successes had opened the door for U.K. R & B music and paved the way for the likes of The Animals (from Newcastle) and The Spencer Davis Group (from Birmingham). With both Liverpool and London docklands doing a roaring trade in the import of black American Motown records, The Beatles and The Searchers were instrumental in popularising the music of their own idols and their personal endorsement was sufficient to catalyse the release of U.S. Motown hits in the U.K.

As 1965 approached, The Who, The Hollies, The Kinks, Herman's Hermits and The Yardbirds were well established as regular chart names. However, America had already begun to fight back. The U.S. reaction to Beatlemania was initially spearheaded by producer Phil Spector's ingenious 'wall of sound' productions which made The Ronettes, The Crystals, The Righteous Brothers and Ike & Tina Turner into household names during a purple sales patch spanning the years 1963 to 1966.

The Beach Boys, The Four Seasons and The Supremes all fought their corner for America throughout 1965, with mixed success. The Four Seasons had first hit the charts with *Sherry* in 1962 and had experienced only sporadic U.K. chart success since, while The Supremes had already set the Tamla Motown juggernaut in motion with *Stop In The Name Of Love*. Meanwhile, The Beach Boys were having problems in flying the Stars & Stripes on a regular basis over here; their three 1965 American top tenners just making the top thirty in Britain.

Conversely, several Americans were attempting to jump on to the British bandwagon in their search of success. Erstwhile chart star Bobby Vee blatantly attempted to clone the British beat sound with the release of *The New Sound From England* LP which contained covers of British hits. The Byrds attempted to sound British on their early releases and The Walker Brothers took up residence in the U.K. to launch their career and use the British connection to propel them to international stardom.

1965 was the year in which the careers of Bob Dylan, Tom Jones and The Moody Blues were established while Petula Clark made a notable chart comeback thanks to the songs and productions of Tony Hatch. The diversity of the charts was shown by the inclusion of The Bachelors, Val Doonican, Ken Dodd and The Seekers alongside Sonny & Cher, Sandie Shaw and Georgie Fame & The Blue Flames.

The year was a good one for the much maligned 'death disc' with *Terry* (by Twinkle) and *Leader Of The Pack* (by The Shangri-Las) both charting while the sombre mood was reinforced with the release of Barry McGuire's *Eve Of Destruction*.

The Beatles and The Rolling Stones continued to dominate the best sellers throughout 1966. In particular, the work of The Beatles had begun to show a new level of maturity, coupling philosophically intriguing lyrics with innovative and complex arrangements.

1966 was the year when The Beach Boys finally repeated their American chart successes on this side of the pond. Highlight of the group's year was unquestionably the release of *Pet Sounds,* an album which had been many months in the planning and represented the culmination of Brian Wilson's undoubted genius. Four hit singles including the chart topping *Good Vibrations* turned the group into America's biggest export since Britain had seized world domination of the pop charts in 1963.

The Kinks perfected their irresistible blend of tongue-in-cheek satire with three moments of absolute Ray Davies brilliance; *Dedicated Follower Of Fashion, Sunny Afternoon* and *Dead End Street* while Small Faces and The Troggs established themselves as major players with four top ten hits apiece. Small Faces were the pin-ups of the mod R&B scene with a raucous live show which played no small part in their elevation to chart prominence while The Troggs carved out a niche in the market for their uniquely raunchy sound and lyrics which were steeped in sexual innuendo.

As light relief to the hard edged sounds of The Rolling Stones, The Kings, Small Faces et al, the two singing Sinatras - Frank and Nancy - hit top spot with *Strangers In The Night* and *These Boots Are Made For Walkin'* respectively. Ironically, father and daughter repeated the achievement as a duo the following year when *Somethin' Stupid* rose to pole position.

One of the best moments of 1966 saw the establishment of Simon & Garfunkel as a major force on the singer songwriter scene. It was in March of that year that the multi-talented duo first clicked; as singers with *Homeward Bound* and as songwriters when The Bachelors of all people gave them a ticket to the charts with their recording of *The Sound Of Silence*.

The Four Tops finally laid to rest the stigma of Tamla Motown being a one artiste label in this country (only The Supremes having hitherto charted in a major way), when *Reach Out I'll Be There* soared to the coveted number one slot. The success of that record opened up the way for an avalanche of Tamla Motown hits in subsequent years, not only for The Four Tops themselves but also for The Supremes, Stevie Wonder, Smokey Robinson & The Miracles and Marvin Gaye amongst others.

1967 represented something of a watershed in popular music. It was the year in which 'pop' was seen to grow up with more meaningful lyrics than ever before. The main catalyst in this transition was undoubtedly the early summer release of *Sergeant Pepper's Lonely Hearts Club Band* by The Beatles. The LP quickly became the jewel in Lennon and McCartney's crown and, with its release, pop music was seen to undergo a metamorphosis, transcending it into an art form in the process. *Sergeant Pepper* combined psychedelia, pop art and virtually all of the period's popular ideals which collectively created a youthful utopia as it epitomised and became the anthem of the 'Summer Of Love' which in turn conveyed its messages of love and peace, sugar coated with sex, drugs and freedom from overburdening parental influences.

Retrospectively, 1967 was a year of somewhat misplaced idealism. Procul Harum (with *A Whiter Shade of Pale* and *Homburg*) and Scott McKenzie (with *San Francisco*) became the voice of the young while Tom Jones and Engelbert Humperdinck redressed the age balance.

Keith West was responsible for one of the most thoughtful pieces of pop during the entire decade as *Excerpt From A Teenage Opera* was shamefully denied number one position by Engelbert Humperdinck's *The Last Waltz,* while Cat Stevens and The Move scored first time chart hits with *Mathew And Son* and *Night Of Fear* respectively. Both releases were on Decca's new trendy Deram record label.

*Massachusetts* gave The Bee Gees their first chart topper while the British beat boom continued to flourish thanks to the ongoing successes of the The Hollies, The Kinks, Manfred Mann and Dave Dee, Dozy, Beaky, Mick & Tich.

Following a brief chart hiatus, America's west coast sound was restored to chart glory thanks to some classic cuts by The Mamas & The Papas and The Turtles. Meanwhile, The Monkees rapidly attained teen idol status as they shot to stardom on the back of a hugely successful television show and a collection of commercially irresistible pop songs which were specifically written to hone the group's teenage appeal.

1968 was the first full year in which Radio One played a part in influencing music tastes. The charts were varied with Love Affair, Crazy World Of Arthur Brown, Esther & Abi Ofarim, Joe Cocker and The Scaffold included amongst the year's chart toppers.

Louis Armstrong topped the charts with *What A Wonderful World* and became the oldest person to do so during the decade. Meanwhile, The Beatles launched their Apple record label and scored immediate hits with their recording of *Hey Jude* and also with the Paul McCartney produced *Those Were The Days* by Mary Hopkin.

Bubblegum music became a force to be reckoned with as Ohio Express (*Yummy Yummy Yummy*) and 1910 Fruitgum Company (*Simon Says*) soared up the best sellers while chart debutantes included such diverse talents as The Bonzo Dog Doo-Dah Band, Don Partridge and Status Quo.

The Beatles, The Rolling Stones, The Beach Boys and The Bee Gees maintained their mass popularity with at least one number one hit apiece.

In the absence of a definitive musical trend the decade limped through its final twelve months aimlessly and devoid of new ideas. Erstwhile chart stars such as The Kinks, Herman's Hermits, The Who and Dave Dee, Dozy, Beaky, Mick & Tich found it a difficult year. Even The Rolling Stones tried just the one crack at the charts with *Honky Tonk Women*. It was the beginning of the end of the significant chart career of Gene Pitney, The Monkees had been and gone, Donovan sank without trace, and many beat groups were playing on borrowed time.

On the positive side, Fleetwood Mac shot to stardom with *Albatross* and singer-songwriter Peter Sarstedt created one of the decade's most durable songs in *Where Do You Go To My Lovely* which deservedly hit top spot during March of that year.

If nothing else, 1969 was memorable for the diversity of chart topping sounds and it is interesting to note that four of the acts never again graced the top twenty. The Archies kept bubblegum alive with *Sugar Sugar,* Zager & Evans hit top spot with the novel studio creation *In The Year 2525,* Thunderclap Newman were believed to have produced a masterpiece with *Something In The Air* while Jane Birkin & Serge Gainsbourg shocked everyone with *Je T'Aime - - - Moi Non Plus.*

The final number one of the year was *Two Little Boys* by Rolf Harris. Hardly the most appropriate of epitaphs for the most creative and innovative decade in the entire history of popular music.

# In 1960 ...

The first record release on the new Warner Brothers record label was *Cathy's Clown* by The Everly Brothers. It was the label's biggest ever chart hit and spent six weeks at the top of the best sellers.

Adam Faith just missed out on a hat-trick of number ones when *Someone Else's Baby* stalled at number two.

**EDDIE COCHRAN** whose career was cut tragically short when he was killed in a road accident on 17th April 1960. His posthumous hit *Three Steps to Heaven* topped the charts in June that year.

Eddie Cochran became the second singer to score a posthumous number one record when *Three Steps To Heaven* hit the top spot. The first was Buddy Holly with *It Doesn't Matter Anymore* in 1959.

Jimmy Jones had two top ten records at the end of June. These were *Handy Man* and *Good Timin'*, the latter of which eventually climbed to the chart's summit. They were the singer's only two hits.

*A Mess Of Blues* became the first Elvis Presley single in two years not to crash into the top ten during the first week of release. It eventually peaked at number two.

The chart of 8th September was one of the few listings to include instrumentals in the top two positions. These were *Apache* (The Shadows) and *Because They're Young* (Duane Eddy).

Roy Orbison's *Only The Lonely* became Sunderland's best selling record during late October, fourteen weeks after being first released. It was the slowest climb to number one during the entire decade.

The theme music of BBC Television's Juke Box Jury, *Hit And Miss* by John Barry, became a Wearside top tenner.

## ADAM FAITH

Cockney Terence Nelhams was born in 1940 and by 1956 was caught up in the Lonnie Donegan inspired skiffle craze when he began performing in The Worried Men. His big break came when he was invited to appear on BBC Television's pop show 6.5 Special. After a couple of flop records, Faith was signed to EMI's Parlophone label and quickly established a trademark of hiccuping vocals, which were strongly reminiscent of Buddy Holly, coupled with exaggerated pronunciation of certain words such as 'bybee' for baby. His first hit *What Do You Want* hit the top of the charts in the early weeks of 1960 and sold in excess of 600,000 copies. The song was written by Les Vandyke (aka Johnny Worth) who went on to write eight of Adam Faith's eleven top ten hits of the sixties. Remarkably, Faith's records rarely exceeded two minutes duration with the first two chart toppers, *What Do You Want* and the similarly sounding *Poor Me*, clocking in at a miserly 1 minute 37 seconds and 1 minute 45 seconds respectively. However, none of this stood in the way of Adam Faith's meteoric rise to the top. Hit records, sell out tours and teen idol status placed him just behind Cliff Richard in the popularity stakes. When the formula sound began to wear thin and the record sales decreased, Faith shrewdly recruited a backing group - The Roulettes - and changed his vocal sound to a hard edged one to bring him into line with the emerging beat group scene. He turned to songwriter Chris Andrews in his search for contemporary recording material and the change in style worked, albeit briefly, notably with the top five hit *The First Time*. By the mid sixties, the hits had dried up and Adam Faith subsequently made a career switch to concentrate on acting.

**BIGGEST 1960 HIT : *What Do You Want.***

**OTHER 60's CHART HITS INCLUDED :**
*Poor Me, Someone Else's Baby, How About That, This Is It, The Time Has Come, As You Like It,*
*Don't That Beat All, The First Time.*

Self-styled independent record producer Joe Meek launched his Triumph record label and immediately charted with *Angela Jones* by Michael Cox.

One of the longest-ever song titles entered the charts in August when Brian Hyland's *Itsy Bitsy Teeny Weeny Yellow Polka Dot Bikini* became a huge summertime hit.

Two early sixties 'standards', *Poetry In Motion* by Johnny Tillotson and *Save The Last Dance For Me* by The Drifters, became end of year hits.

The only live recording to top the charts during the entire decade was Lonnie Donegan's *My Old Man's A Dustman*.

Elvis Presley's *It's Now Or Never* became one of only three sixties records to enter the chart at number one. The other two were *The Young Ones* (Cliff Richard in 1962) and *Get Back* (The Beatles in 1969).

*Ain't Misbehavin'* became Tommy Bruce's only top ten hit.

Although he was predominantly a fifties chart star, NAT KING COLE had significant hits during the sixties including *That's You* (1960), *Let There Be Love* (1962) and *Ramblin' Rose* (1962).

## Wearside Top Ten ~ 5th January 1960

1. What Do You Want To Make Those Eyes At Me For ............... Emile Ford & The Checkmates (Pye)
2. What Do You Want ........................ Adam Faith (Parlophone)
3. Oh! Carol ..................................... Neil Sedaka (RCA)
4. Red River Rock ............. Johnny & The Hurricanes (London)
5. Travelling Light ............................. Cliff Richard (Columbia)
6. Wild Cat ..................................... Gene Vincent (Capitol)
7. Starry Eyed ............................ Michael Holliday (Columbia)
8. Teen Beat ..................................... Sandy Nelson (Top Rank)
9. Bad Boy ..................................... Marty Wilde (Philips)
10. Poison Ivy ..................................... The Coasters (London)

## Wearside Top Ten ~ 15th March 1960

1. *Running Bear* ................................ Johnny Preston (Mercury)
2. *Poor Me* .......................................... Adam Faith (Parlophone)
3. *You Got What It Takes* ..................... Marv Johnson (London)
4. *Who Could Be Bluer* ..................... Jerry Lordan (Parlophone)
5. *On A Slow Boat To China* ........................................................
   Emile Ford & The Checkmates (Pye)
6. *Delaware* .................................... Perry Como (RCA)
7. *Why* .................................................. Anthony Newley (Decca)
8. *Hit And Miss* ..................................... John Barry (Columbia)
9. *Pretty Blue Eyes* ........................... Craig Douglas (Top Rank)
10. *Summer Set* ................................. Mr. Acker Bilk (Columbia)

Sam Cooke hit the charts with the first of three classic hits when *Chain Gang* made the top ten. Subsequent top tenners for the American star were *Cupid* (1961) and *Twistin' The Night Away* (1962).

After making the top ten with *You Got What It Takes*, Marv Johnson had to wait a further nine years for his next major hit *I'll Pick A Rose For My Rose*.

The pick of entertainment in Sunderland included dancing to Al Flush & His Orchestra at The Rink or to Billy Carr & His Orchestra at Seaburn Hall.

Sunderland's top pop concert in 1960 was at the Odeon Cinema on 10th April when Cliff Richard topped the bill. He was supported by Frank Ifield and Kathy Kirby who were both still relatively unknown at the time. Top seat price was 7s 6d.

One of the first chart acts of the decade to visit Sunderland was
CLIFF RICHARD & THE SHADOWS, who, at the time were
riding high with *Voice In The Wilderness*.

## THE SHADOWS

Originally The Drifters and Cliff Richard's backing group, the instrumental line up of Hank Marvin, Bruce Welch, Jet Harris and Tony Meehan changed their name to The Shadows in July 1959 and proceeded to become the U.K.'s premier instrumental outfit of the sixties. The group enjoyed an incredible run of fourteen top ten hits (including five number ones) during the early to mid sixties and by 1961 they had moved away from simply being Cliff Richard's backing group to establishing themselves as major recording and concert artists in their own right. Following their successes as backing musicians on Cliff Richard's early discs, Columbia Records' A & R manager Norrie Paramor signed the group to a recording deal. Soon afterwards they met singer-songwriter Jerry Lordan who offered them first refusal on a new number, *Apache*. The Shadows recorded the track and it gave them their biggest ever chart hit, peaking at number one and staying on the charts for twenty one weeks. Tony Meehan left the group in October 1961 (to be replaced by Brian Bennett) and was followed by Jet Harris in April 1962 (to be replaced by Brian Locking) but the change in personnel failed to halt The Shadows' onslaught on the charts. The group continued to work with Cliff Richard in films without appearing to lose any of their credibility as serious musicians. Almost uniquely, The Shadows enjoyed the duality of a modern generation chart group whilst remaining part of the showbiz establishment. The run of sixties hits finally dried up in 1967 although they experienced something of a renaissance in subsequent decades.

**BIGGEST 1960 HIT : Apache.**

**OTHER 60'S CHART HITS INCLUDED :**
**Man Of Mystery, Frightened City, Kon-Tiki, Wonderful Land, Guitar Tango, Dance On, Foot Tapper, Atlantis.**

## NEIL SEDAKA

Neil Sedaka was born on 13th March 1939 in Brooklyn, New York and began his songwriting career when he teamed up with Howard Greenfield in the early fifties. He was briefly a member of The Tokens before winning a scholarship to the Julliard School Of Music in New York where he trained as a classical pianist. In 1958, top songwriters Pomus and Shuman put Neil and Howard in contact with the principals of the famous Brill Building in New York where they were signed to an exclusive songwriting contract. One of their first songs, *Stupid Cupid*, was a worldwide hit for Connie Francis and soon afterwards Sedaka signed a recording contract with RCA. His second record release on RCA, *I Go Ape*, was a wild rocker and was a substantial hit. The next chart record was *Oh! Carol* and was written for Neil's former girlfriend Carole King. The record was released in late 1959 and reached number three on the charts in 1960 during a seventeen week chart run. The Sedaka - Greenfield writing partnership was one of the most successful of the early sixties and made Neil Sedaka into a household name. The songs were expertly crafted and wonderfully encapsulated the emotional experiences of teenage love of a more innocent time. Sedaka was the epitomy of the clean-cut American teen balladeer who, along with many of his counterparts, suffered a rapid decline in chart fortunes following the emergence of British beat groups in 1963. By 1966 Sedaka briefly abandoned the role of pop star to successfully concentrate on songwriting. He re-established himself as a contemporary performer in 1972 and has remained a major concert attraction ever since.

**BIGGEST 1960 HIT : Oh! Carol.**

**OTHER 60's CHART HITS INCLUDED : Stairway To Heaven, Calendar Girl, Little Devil, Happy Birthday Sweet Sixteen, King Of Clowns, Breaking Up Is Hard To Do, Next Door To An Angel, Let's Go Steady Again.**

### *Wearside Top Ten ~ 31st May 1960*

1. *Cathy's Clown* .............. The Everly Brothers (Warner Bros.)
2. *Sweet Nothin's* ................................... Brenda Lee (Brunswick)
3. *Cradle Of Love* ........................... Johnny Preston (Mercury)
4. *Handy Man* ................................................ Jimmy Jones (MGM)
5. *Mama* .................................................. Connie Francis (MGM)
6. *Someone Else's Baby* ..................... Adam Faith (Parlophone)
7. *I Wanna Go Home* .............................. Lonnie Donegan (Pye)
8. *Stairway To Heaven* ................................. Neil Sedaka (RCA)
9. *The Heart Of A Teenage Girl* ....... Craig Douglas (Top Rank)
10. *Let The Little Girl Dance* .................... Billy Bland (London)

### *Wearside Top Ten ~ 9th August 1960*

1. *Please Don't Tease* ......................... Cliff Richard (Columbia)
2. *Apache* .............................................. The Shadows (Columbia)
3. *Shakin' All Over* ............. Johnny Kidd & The Pirates (HMV)
4. *The Girl Of My Best Friend/A Mess of Blues* ......................... Elvis Presley (RCA)
5. *Itsy Bitsy Teeny Weeny Yellow Polka Dot Bikini* ..................... Brian Hyland (London)
6. *Good Timin'* .......................................... Jimmy Jones (MGM)
7. *Love Is Like A Violin* ................................. Ken Dodd (Decca)
8. *He'll Have To Go* ..................................... Jim Reeves (RCA)
9. *Ain't Misbehavin'* ......................... Tommy Bruce (Columbia)
10. *If She Should Come To You* ............ Anthony Newley (Decca)

# THE EVERLY BROTHERS

Don and Phil Everly were born in 1937 and 1939 respectively and from their early years appeared on their parents' radio shows. The brothers' crystal clear harmonies made them an instant success on record and before the end of the fifties they had already notched up six chart hits including the number one hit *All I Have To Do Is Dream*. Their early successes ensured access to some of the top songwriters of the era including the works of Felice & Boudleaux Bryant, Carole King, Gerry Goffin, John D. Loudermilk and Howard Greenfield. Their earliest hits were released on the New York based Cadence record label which were distributed in this country by Decca Records on their black and silver London label. In 1960, The Everly Brothers signed a one million dollar deal with the newly formed Warner Brothers Records and released the Don Everly song *Cathy's Clown*. By Everly's standards the song was a big production job with gutsy echo laden harmonies which sounded quite different from any of their previous recordings. The record stormed to the top of the charts where it stayed for eight weeks during which time it sold in excess of one million copies in the U.K. and gave the brothers their biggest ever hit. The hits continued at a cracking pace until 1963 when the Everly's star dimmed with the arrival of the British beat boom although they did have one further major hit left in them; *The Price of Love* briefly restoring them to the top ten in 1965. Thereafter the hits dried up and personal conflict between Don and Phil appeared to signal the end of the act although The Everly Brothers re-surfaced during the eighties as a live act on the nostalgia concert circuit.

> *BIGGEST 1960 HIT : Cathy's Clown*
>
> *OTHER 60'S CHART HITS INCLUDED :*
> *When Will I Be Loved, Walk Right Back, Temptation, Cryin' In The Rain, How Can I Meet Her,*
> *No One Can Make My Sunshine Smile, The Price Of Love.*

## Wearside Top Ten ~ 27th September 1960

1. Tell Laura I Love Her ................. Ricky Valance (Columbia)
2. Only The Lonely ............................ Roy Orbison (London)
3. The Girl Of My Best Friend/A Mess Of Blues ...................... Elvis Presley (RCA)
4. Apache ........................... The Shadows (Columbia)
5. Nine Times Out Of Ten ................. Cliff Richard (Columbia)
6. So Sad/Lucille ............... The Everly Brothers (Warner Bros.)
7. Walk Don't Run .......................... The Ventures (Top Rank)
8. Because They're Young .......................... Duane Eddy (RCA)
9. As Long As He Needs Me ........... Shirley Bassey (Columbia)
10. How About That .......................... Adam Faith (Parlophone)

## Wearside Top Ten ~ 20th December 1960

1. It's Now Or Never ................................ Elvis Presley (RCA)
2. Save The Last Dance For Me ............ The Drifters (London)
3. I Love You ...................................... Cliff Richard (Columbia)
4. Poetry In Motion ......................... Johnny Tillotson (London)
5. As Long As He Needs Me ........... Shirley Bassey (Columbia)
6. Little Donkey .......................... Nina & Frederick (Columbia)
7. Counting Teardrops ..... Emile Ford & The Checkmates (Pye)
8. Lonely Pup (In A Christmas Shop) ............................... Adam Faith (Parlophone)
9. My Heart Has A Mind Of Its Own .... Connie Francis (MGM)
10. My Love For You .......................... Johnny Mathis (Fontana)

# DUANE EDDY

The King of 'twang' created his legendary sound by recording the bass strings of a Grestch guitar through an echo chamber. Eddy had a string of chart hits spanning the late fifties to early sixties, most were co-written with record producer Lee Hazelwood and most followed a tried and tested formula. In the U.S., Duane Eddy was signed to the then fledgling Jamie label (whose releases were put out in the U.K. on Decca's London American label) for whom he soon attained superstar status. *Peter Gunn Theme* gave Eddy his first top ten hit in 1959 but the early sixties were his most productive era with two hits in each of 1960, 1961 and 1962. His backing group, The Rebel Rousers, had an equally distinctive sound with prominent saxophone also a feature of most of the hits. In 1962, Eddy changed allegiance when he left Jamie for the giant RCA Victor and it was with this record label that he broke with tradition and recorded a number with lyrics sung by the newly formed female backing group The Rebelettes. The song was (*Dance With The*) *Guitar Man* and it was to be his last hit of the decade before he was nudged out of the spotlight by the British beat boom. There were two brief returns to chart activity, one each in the seventies and eighties but, apart from the occasional appearance on revival packages, Duane Eddy has kept a comparatively low profile since his halcyon chart days.

> *BIGGEST 1960 HIT : Because They're Young.*
>
> *OTHER 60's CHART HITS INCLUDED :*
> *Shazam, Pepe, Theme From Dixie, Ballad Of Paladin, (Dance With The) Guitar Man.*

The exceptionally talented BOBBY DARIN
who hit the top ten on seven occasions during the sixties.

# BOBBY DARIN

In an early interview Bobby Darin boldly predicted that one day he would aspire to legendary status. Darin was born Walden Robert Cassotto on 14th March 1936 in New York. Following a spell making jingles for television commercials, he met up and coming writer/showbiz entrepreneur Don Kirshner and soon landed a major recording contract. His earliest attempts to scale the pop charts were unsuccessful but his fortunes changed dramatically in 1958 when he scored a hit with *Splish Splash*. By the start of the sixties Darin had scored two number ones, the superbly commercial *Dream Lover* and the finger-clicking cabaret masterpiece *Mack The Knife*. Bobby Darin never sought the identikit image of the teen idol, he refused to allow his music to be categorised and he had the outstanding vocal ability to tackle a variety of contemporary styles. His choice of material for singles during the early sixties ably demonstrated that point. From the brassy, swinging arrangement of the jazz orientated *Bill Bailey* to the semi-comedy out-and-out pop of *Multiplication;* all bore the Darin hallmark of class. By 1962 Bobby Darin was sharing his time between singing and acting careers with box office successes in the latter area via roles in Come September, Hell Is For Heroes and Pressure Point. After four years away from the pop charts, he re-surfaced in yet another musical guise, this time with a distinctive interpretation of *If I Were A Carpenter*. Darin had suffered from a weak heart since a childhood attack of rheumatic fever and once said that he didn't think he would make thirty. He died in 1973 during open heart surgery, aged thirty seven. His earlier prediction that he would become a legend was spot on.

> **BIGGEST 1960 HIT : Clementine.**
>
> **OTHER 60's CHART HITS INCLUDED :**
> **La Mer (Beyond The Sea), Lazy River, Multiplication, Things, If I Were A Carpenter.**

# The Ones That Got Away In ...

*Puppy Love* ........................................ Paul Anka
*Bill Bailey* ...................................... Bobby Darin
*Mountain Of Love* ....................................... Kenny Lynch
*Broken Doll* ................................................ Tommy Bruce
*I Just Go For You* ....................................... Jimmy Jones
*Wondrous Place* ............................................. Billy Fury
*Four Little Heels* ......................................... Brian Hyland

By the end of 1959 Paul Anka had scored an impressive six top ten hits in little over two years and when *Puppy Love* climbed to number two in America, further British chart success seemed assured. Amazingly, the record did not even enter the top thirty and Anka failed to hit the top ten throughout the sixties.

Likewise, *Bill Bailey* by Bobby Darin failed to live up to chart expectations although in Darin's case the disappointment represented only a brief chart hiatus.

By 1960 Billy Fury was well on his way to legendary status when he released *Wondrous Place;* one of his personal favourites. Retrospectively regarded as an early sixties classic, the record deserved so much more than its modest top thirty placing.

# In 1961 ...

One of the year's biggest hits was *Are You Sure* by The Allisons which was also the United Kingdom's entry in the Eurovision Song Contest. It was voted into second position.

Connie Francis benefitted from the songwriting talents of Neil Sedaka with both sides of her chartbuster *Where The Boys Are/Baby Roo* being composed by Sedaka.

*LEFT*
The South Shields record shop of Leslie Saville ran a weekly advertisement in The South Shields Gazette throughout the sixties.

*RIGHT*
All American girl CONNIE FRANCIS whose biggest hit of the year was the double sided *Where The Boys Are/Baby Roo* both of which were Neil Sedaka compositions.

Tony Orlando had his one and only hit as a solo performer when *Bless You* hit the charts during the autumn months. Orlando subsequently re-surfaced during the early seventies as lead singer with chart group Dawn.

It was the era of cover versions. At that time, many chart hits which were not American recordings, were British 'cover' versions of U.S. hits. In some cases both the original American recording and the British cover version would appear simultaneously on the charts. There were three examples of this early in the year with *Rubber Ball* (original by Bobby Vee and cover by Marty Wilde), *Pepe* (original by Duane Eddy and cover by Russ Conway) and *Sailor* (two British versions by Petula Clark and Anne Shelton).

---

## CLIFF RICHARD

Cliff Richard was born in India as Harry Roger Webb in 1940 and began performing Rock & Roll music in 1957. He worked in a trio - The Drifters - at various clubs in Hertfordshire before graduating to the 21's coffee bar in London at which point the act expanded to a quartet. There then followed a Gaumont Cinema talent contest, a demo tape to Columbia Records' Norrie Paramor and a meeting with television producer Jack Good, all of which combined to bring about the release of *Move It*. With the benefit of a carefully constructed media campaign, the record duly gave Richard his first chart hit at which point he was paraded around the country as a hip-swinging sex symbol. By this time, the line-up of The Drifters had been revised and the name changed to The Shadows. Following some mediocre, moderately selling Rock & Roll singles, Richard's career took a MOR turn with the recording of *Living Doll* in 1959. This paved the way for a run of commercial pop successes during the sixties and well beyond and a longevity unprecedented in popular music. Thirty three top ten hits represented the decade's high spots; the films, Saturday night television shows and Eurovision represented the low spots in the eyes of many observers. The banality of some of Richard's lyrics and the latter day 'too good to be true' image meant that a sizeable proportion of the population could never take Cliff Richard's music seriously. That said, no performer has lasted the course better than Cliff Richard and to transcend from fifties teen-rebel to nineties housewives' choice, with thirty three 60's hits in between, cannot be bad for someone not blessed with an obvious abundance of talent.

**BIGGEST 1961 HIT : *Theme For A Dream*.**

**OTHER 60's CHART HITS INCLUDED :**
*The Young Ones, Bachelor Boy, Summer Holiday, It's All In The Game, The Minute You're Gone, Congratulations.*

The 'luxury ballroom with popular prices' in 1961.

It was also the time of the 'double sided hit'; that is, a record with an equally strong song on either side. The first sixties double sided chart hit was *Ebony Eyes/Walk Right Back* by the Everly Brothers.

Eden Kane's debut record, the Cadbury's sponsored *Hot Chocolate Crazy* was not a hit. The next single was *Well I Ask You* and it fared much better than its predecessor when it became the best selling single during the first week of August.

## EDEN KANE

Shortly after eighteen year old Indian-born Richard Graham Sarstedt changed his name to Eden Kane, he was dubbed 'The Beau Brummel Of Popsters'. That was in 1960 when Kane's first big showbiz break came after winning a Cadbury's sponsored talent contest which led to the release of his first single *Hot Chocolate Crazy* on Pye Records. The record was not a hit but the seeds had been sown to mould Eden Kane into one of the first home produced heart-throbs of the sixties. By 1961 he was signed to Decca Records and in the summer of that year stormed to the number one position with the catchy Les Vandyke song *Well I Ask You* which was the first of four straight top ten hits. The fourth hit, *I Don't Know Why*, was a revival of the old standard which was chosen as a single after Eden's performance of the song on The Big Star Show of 1962 tour (which also starred Billy Fury and John Leyton) regularly won standing ovations. Kane's career then suffered a serious setback when his management company folded in late 1962. Attempts to salvage hit records from the wreckage failed when both *House To Let* and *Sounds Funny To Me* failed to make even the top fifty charts. A new management deal in 1963 secured him a recording contract with Fontana for whom his third single became a hit the following year. The song was the wonderfully atmospheric *Boys Cry* which, despite some creditable follow-ups, proved to be Eden Kane's final chart entry. He subsequently emigrated, firstly to Australia and then to America and was inactive on the British pop music scene for many years although he did record a 'one-off' single, *Walking In The Sand,* with brothers Peter and Robin Sarstedt in 1966. In recent years he has re-emerged on nostalgia package tours with many of his sixties contemporaries.

*BIGGEST 1961 HIT : Well I Ask You.*

*OTHER 60'S CHART HITS INCLUDED :*
*Get Lost, Forget Me Not, I Don't Know Why, Boys Cry.*

## ELVIS PRESLEY

For most of the sixties, Elvis Aaron Presley was spoken of in revered terms by his vast army of fans and there can be no denying that the American rock legend had earlier established himself as the most significant pop music phenomenon of his era. After several record releases on the Sun label in the U.S.A., Colonel Tom Parker took over the management of Elvis' career in 1955 and soon placed his protege with RCA Records. His first record for the label, *Heartbreak Hotel,* was an immediate best seller and thereafter followed an impressive run of eighteen top tenners, including four number ones, during the mid to late fifties. Such was Presley's immense popularity that even a two year stint in the U.S. Army failed to act as a hiatus to his career. The turn of the decade was Elvis' most successful period. He was released from the U.S. Army in March 1960, hit the charts with *Stuck On You* the following month and embarked upon a run of twelve top ten hits, nine of which made number one, ending with the Christmas 1962 chart topper *Return To Sender*. It was at this time that Tom Parker concentrated Presley's career on film making and as a consequence most of his recordings were of the soundtrack variety which failed to impress the record buying public. During a four year period from late 1963 Presley released an incredible twenty three singles but only three made the top ten. Whether it was bad management direction or a declining artistic talent which resulted in Presley's fall from grace, his lack of mid sixties success cannot be ignored when considering his alleged omnipotence during the swinging decade. The popularity decline was arrested in the late sixties and the seventies saw a return to mass popularity before Elvis Presley's untimely death in 1977.

*BIGGEST 1961 HIT : Are You Lonesome Tonight.*

*OTHER 60's CHART HITS INCLUDED :*
*It's Now Or Never, His Latest Flame, Good Luck Charm, She's Not You, Return To Sender,*
*Devil In Disguise, Crying In The Chapel.*

Self-styled independent record producer Joe Meek experienced his first of three sixties chart toppers when John Leyton's *Johnny Remember Me* hit the number one spot in September.

The top ten chart of 2nd October featured four female vocalists for the only time during the early sixties. These were Shirley Bassey (*Reach For The Stars*), Connie Francis (*Together*), Cleo Laine (*You'll Answer To Me*) and Helen Shapiro (*Don't Treat Me Like A Child*).

Acker Bilk's *Stranger On The Shore* made its chart debut and became the region's longest running best seller of the decade.

There were four chart toppers for Elvis Presley; *Are You Lonesome Tonight, Wooden Heart, Surrender* and the double 'A' sided *His Latest Flame/Little Sister* making it his joint best year for number ones.

Chart debutant Del Shannon scored the only number one of his career with *Runaway*.

The Shadows had their best ever chart year with four top ten entries; *FBI, Frightened City, Kon-Tiki* and *The Savage*.

There was a top twenty debut for The Springfields with *Bambino*.

THE EVERLY BROTHERS

Don and Phil, THE EVERLY BROTHERS, who were prolific hit makers during the late fifties and early sixties.

Singer-Songwriter DEL SHANNON whose debut hit *Runaway* topped the hit parade in July 1961.

## DEL SHANNON

Del Shannon came into the world as Charles Westover on 30th December 1934 in Michigan, U.S.A. He made his debut as a performer on the Get Up And Go forces radio show while in the military in West Germany. His earliest songwriting efforts led to a recording deal with Big Top Records and the eventual release of his first record in 1961. *Runaway* topped the charts in both the U.S.A. and U.K. Shannon's successes in his native country were overshadowed by his popularity in the U.K. where he scored hit after hit with his own compositions, most of which had a sombre lyrical content with tales of unfaithfulness, broken hearts, misery and inevitable loneliness. Del Shannon's highly distinctive falsetto vocals established him as one of America's hottest exports and he toured the U.K. regularly in the early sixties during which time he clocked up a run of ten consecutive hit singles. As well as writing/co-writing his own material, Shannon involved himself with the production of his records. After 1963, his appearances on the charts became less frequent as he suffered from the same fate as many of his American contemporaries in the wake of Beatlemania. He was to enjoy one final moment of chart glory in 1965 in one of his finest hours with *Keep Searchin'*, a spectacular big sounding production loaded with all the familiar sounding Shannon trademarks from past successes. Thereafter the hits dried up although he did maintain a sizeable British fan base and continued to tour well into the seventies. Sadly, on 8th February 1990 the purveyor of songs which almost glorified failure and despair performed the ultimate enactment of his lyrics when he pointed a rifle to his head and pulled the trigger.

*BIGGEST 1961 HIT : Runaway.*

*OTHER 60's CHART HITS INCLUDED :*
*Hats Off To Larry, Hey Little Girl, Swiss Maid, Little Town Flirt, Two Kinds Of Teardrops,*
*Keep Searchin' (We'll Follow The Sun).*

## Wearside Top Ten ~ 28th February 1961

1. Walk Right Back/Ebony Eyes ........................... The Everly Brothers (Warner Bros.)
2. Will You Still Love Me Tomorrow ........................ The Shirelles (Top Rank)
3. Sailor ........................................................... Petula Clark (Pye)
4. Riders In The Sky ............................ The Ramrods (London)
5. Are You Sure ...................................... The Allisons (Fontana)
6. Calendar Girl .......................................... Neil Sedaka (RCA)
7. Who Am I .................................................. Adam Faith (Parlophone)
8. Pepe ...................................................... Duane Eddy (London)
9. Buona Sara ....................................... Mr. Acker Bilk (Columbia)
10. Baby Sittin' Boogie ......................... Buzz Clifford (Fontana)

## Wearside Top Ten ~ 17th April 1961

1. Wooden Heart ......................................... Elvis Presley (RCA)
2. Lazy River .......................................... Bobby Darin (London)
3. Are You Sure ..................................... The Allisons (Fontana)
4. Walk Right Back ........... The Everly Brothers (Warner Bros.)
5. Theme For A Dream ....................... Cliff Richard (Columbia)
6. My Kind Of Girl ........................... Matt Monro (Parlophone)
7. FBI .................................................. The Shadows (Columbia)
8. You're Driving Me Crazy ..................................................... The Temperance Seven (Parlophone)
9. Where The Boys Are/Baby Roo ......... Connie Francis (MGM)
10. Blue Moon ................................................. The Marcels (Pye)

Teen idol BOBBY VEE with five top ten hits during 1961 to his credit including the million seller *Take Good Care Of My Baby.*

# BOBBY VEE

The career of sixteen year old Robert Thomas Velline received its first real boost in highly macabre circumstances. It was in 1959 that Vee's group The Shadows were asked to deputise for Buddy Holly after the singer was killed in an aeroplane crash. Soon afterwards Bobby Vee was introduced to successful record producer 'Snuff' Garrett at which point he assumed solo artist status. With his well groomed boy-next-door looks, Bobby Vee's talents were the perfect vehicle for the plethora of boy meets girl teen anthems which were dripping from the pens of the famous Brill Building songwriters during the early sixties. The highly infectious Gene Pitney composition *Rubber Ball* gave Vee his first taste of British chart success in January 1961. The record became a million seller and made Bobby Vee into a teen idol. Over the next three years he could do no wrong as he enjoyed hit after hit with his pick of the new songs. He charted with three LP's, *Bobby Vee Meets The Crickets, A Forever Kind Of Love* and *A Bobby Vee Recording Session,* while his frequent British tours, television and radio appearances and cameo roles in the films Play It Cool and Just For Fun secured him a strong fan base. He charted briefly in 1963 with *Bobby Tomorrow* after which he lost the midas touch and the hits dried up as the beat groups took a stranglehold on the charts. Bobby Vee continued to release records on a regular basis until the late sixties including an LP *Bobby Vee Sings The New Sound From England* which featured his versions of British hits as well as spawning a new song *She's Sorry* which was a copycat version of *She Loves You*. He re-surfaced as a concert attraction in Britain during the eighties, mainly on nostalgia package tours.

**BIGGEST 1961 HIT : Take Good Care Of My Baby.**

**OTHER 60's CHART HITS INCLUDED :**
**Rubber Ball, More Than I Can Say, Run To Him, Sharing You, How Many Tears, The Night Has A Thousand Eyes.**

**HELEN SHAPIRO who first hit the top ten as a fourteen year old in 1961 with *Don't Treat Me Like A Child*.**

# HELEN SHAPIRO

Helen Shapiro became an overnight singing sensation when she burst on to the scene - and the top ten charts - as a fourteen year old in 1961. Her mature singing voice brought her to the attention of Norrie Paramor, A & R manager at Columbia Records who immediately signed her to a recording contract. The appropriate lyric on her debut *Don't Treat Me Like A Child* resulted in appearances on top television and radio programmes and the record rocketed up the charts where it took up residency for twenty weeks. Shapiro's next two releases both topped the U.K. charts and established her in numerous overseas territories. She became the first British female singer to make over a dozen television and radio appearances before her fifteenth birthday. Upon leaving school at fifteen, she began a hectic touring schedule which included a season at the London Palladium and was voted 'Best British Female Singer'. The hits continued to come thick and fast well into 1962 when suddenly, and without warning, her name all but disappeared from the charts. With the beat group revolution gathering pace, Helen Shapiro suffered from the public perception of belonging to an earlier era despite still being a mere sixteen years old. Her sudden fall from grace was inexplicable considering the quality of her later singles. *Keep Away From Other Girls*, *Queen For Tonight* and *Woe Is Me* all deserved high chart placings but just managed to briefly scrape into the lower reaches of the top forty. As the decade progressed, Shapiro drifted towards jazz orientated material with which she established herself as a respected performer.

> **BIGGEST 1961 HIT : *Walkin' Back To Happiness*.**
>
> **OTHER 60's CHART HITS INCLUDED :**
> ***Don't Treat Me Like A Child, You Don't Know,***
> ***Tell Me What He Said, Little Miss Lonely.***

ohnny Tillotson's clean cut vocals ensured number one status for *Poetry In Motion* during the second week of the year. Despite a further five hits, none progressed as far as the top ten.

La Strada became South Shields' first night club when it opened early in the new year.

## *Wearside Top Ten ~ 19th June 1961*

1. *Surrender* ................................ Elvis Presley (RCA)
2. *Runaway* ................................ Del Shannon (London)
3. *Halfway To Paradise* ............................. Billy Fury (Decca)
4. *Hello Mary Lou* ............................... Ricky Nelson (London)
5. *Little Devil* ................................ Neil Sedaka (RCA)
6. *Temptation* .................... The Everly Brothers (Warner Bros.)
7. *More Than I Can Say* ........................... Bobby Vee (London)
8. *Running Scared* ................................ Roy Orbison (London)
9. *Well I Ask You* ........................................ Eden Kane (Decca)
10. *Don't Treat Me Like A Child* ........ Helen Shapiro (Columbia)

## *Wearside Top Ten ~ 4th September 1961*

1. *Johnny Remember Me* ................... John Leyton (Top Rank)
2. *You Don't Know* .......................... Helen Shapiro (Columbia)
3. *Reach For The Stars* ................... Shirley Bassey (Columbia)
4. *Well I Ask You* ......................................... Eden Kane (Decca)
5. *Romeo* ...................................................... Petula Clark (Pye)
6. *Marcheta* .............................................. Karl Denver (Decca)
7. *That's My Home* ....................... Mr. Acker Bilk (Columbia)
8. *How Many Tears* ...................................... Bobby Vee (London)
9. *Cupid* ................................................... Sam Cooke (RCA)
10. *Don't You Know It* ....................... Adam Faith (Parlophone)

## Wearside Top Ten ~ 16th October 1961

1. *Walkin' Back To Happiness* ......... Helen Shapiro (Columbia)
2. *Jealousy* ...................................................... Billy Fury (Decca)
3. *Kon-Tiki* ........................................ The Shadows (Columbia)
4. *Michael* ...................................... The Highwaymen (HMV)
5. *Wild Wind* ........................................ John Leyton (Top Rank)
6. *Hats Off To Larry* ........................... Del Shannon (London)
7. *Together* ........................................ Connie Francis (MGM)
8. *Bless You* ...................................... Tony Orlando (Fontana)
9. *Get Lost* ............................................ Eden Kane (Decca)
10. *Sucu Sucu* ........................... Laurie Johnson Orchestra (Pye)

## Wearside Top Ten ~ 28th December 1961

1. *Moon River* ...................................... Danny Williams (HMV)
2. *Tower Of Strength* ........................ Frankie Vaughan (Philips)
3. *Midnight In Moscow* ................................. Kenny Ball (Pye)
4. *Let There Be Drums* ........................ Sandy Nelson (London)
5. *Johnny Will* ............................................ Pat Boone (London)
6. *Stranger On The Shore* ............... Mr. Acker Bilk (Columbia)
7. *Take Good Care Of My Baby* ............... Bobby Vee (London)
8. *Happy Birthday Sweet Sixteen* ............... Neil Sedaka (RCA)
9. *Multiplication* ..................................... Bobby Darin (London)
10. *Big Bad John* ....................................... Jimmy Dean (Philips)

Two of the year's distinctly different hits were consecutive chart toppers; *On The Rebound* (Floyd Cramer) and *You're Driving Me Crazy* (The Temperance Seven).

Ricky Nelson scored his biggest selling British hit with the double sided *Hello Mary Lou/Travellin' Man*.

## *The Ones That Got Away In ...*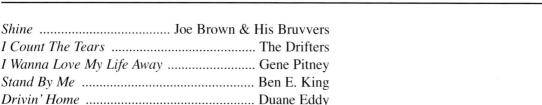

*Shine* .................................... Joe Brown & His Bruvvers
*I Count The Tears* ........................................ The Drifters
*I Wanna Love My Life Away* ........................ Gene Pitney
*Stand By Me* ................................................ Ben E. King
*Drivin' Home* ............................................... Duane Eddy
*Cryin'* ........................................................ Roy Orbison
*Everlovin'* .................................................. Ricky Nelson

*I Count The Tears* was a minor gem from the pens of Pomus-Shuman and was released as the follow up to *Save The Last Dance For Me*. With a catchy hookline and a superb string arrangement, the record was expected to emulate the success of its predecessor but it fell well short of doing that.

Gene Pitney's up-tempo *I Wanna Love My Life Away* was far removed from his subsequent big selling mid sixties ballads. It gave him his U.K. chart debut but had the song been recorded by a better known artist it would have surely climbed higher than its number twenty six peak.

Meanwhile, Roy Orbison's dramatic ballad *Cryin'* could only manage to climb as high as number twenty five and the song did not realise its full sales potential until Don McLean took it to the top of the charts in 1980.

# In 1962 ...

*Theme From Z Cars* by Johnny Keating shot into the Wearside Top Ten and was soon adopted by Sunderland A.F.C. as its match day theme music.

*Happy Birthday Sweet Sixteen* by Neil Sedaka became one of the fastest selling singles of the year and gave the American singer-songwriter his sixth chart hit.

The best selling instrumental hit of the decade, *Wonderful Land* by The Shadows, spent eight weeks at number one.

Wendy Richards' first claim to fame was in 1962 when she dueted with Mike Sarne on *Come Outside*. The record reached number one on the charts in June 1962.

Adam Faith was the only sixties artist to take a song with a Shakespeare play title into the charts. *As You Like It* was a summer 1962 hit for Mr. Faith whose feat was repeated in subsequent decades by Dire Straits (*Romeo and Juliet*) and David Essex (*A Winter's Tale*).

How many of these stars can you name from this 1962 advertisement in popular music newspaper Disc.

---

## BRIAN HYLAND

New Yorker Brian Hyland first shot to stardom as a sixteen year old in the summer of 1960 with the novelty hit *Itsy Bitsy Teeny Weeny Yellow Polka Dot Bikini*. Two further novelty records that year were less successful. The follow-up single *Four Little Heels* was only a minor hit while the next release, *Lop-Sided Overloaded And It Wiggled When We Rode It*, was a worldwide flop. In 1961, Hyland left the Kapp label in America (London label in Britain) for the larger ABC Paramount label (via HMV in Britain), changed his image to the all American boy and changed his musical direction to encompass crooning ballads which were more suited to his vocal abilities. Hyland's new dreamboat status coupled with the specially created teen love songs of Gary Geld and Peter Udell simply could not miss. 1962 was Brian Hyland's best year. It was the year when he rode the crest of a popularity wave with three classic songs of adolescent romance. *Ginny Come Lately, Sealed With A Kiss* and *Warmed Over Kisses (Left Over Love)* tugged at the heart strings of the female teen population. There would surely have been further formula hits had it not been for the rapid switch in musical tastes during 1963 when Brian Hyland and his ballads became passé overnight. Hyland continued recording and the likes of *If Mary's There, I May Not Live To See Tomorrow* and *Let Us Make Our Own Mistakes* deserved a chart placing but were largely ignored. There was a brief renaissance in 1975 when *Sealed With A Kiss* became a hit for the second time around.

> **BIGGEST 1962 HIT : Sealed With A Kiss.**
>
> **OTHER 60's CHART HITS INCLUDED :**
> *Itsy Bitsy Teeny Weeny Yellow Polka Dot Bikini, Ginny Come Lately, Warmed Over Kisses (Left Over Love).*

---

*RIGHT*
A typical early sixties touring package.

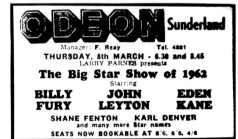

*LEFT*
Early sixties recording stars on a visit to Stockton in 1962.

# CHRIS MONTEZ

In early 1963, Chris Montez toured the U.K. and headlined above The Beatles. The star billing came as a result of his global, million selling hit *Let's Dance* which peaked at number two on the Wearside chart of November 1962. Christopher Montanez was born in 1943 and began singing and writing songs as a star-struck fifteen year old. He was spotted by talent-seeking record producer Jim Lee who duly released Montez first record *All You Had To Do Was Tell Me* which became a localised U.S. hit. Encouraged by the sales of that first record, Lee penned the Ritchie Valens inspired *Let's Dance* and co-penned the top ten follow-up, *Some Kinda Fun,* with the artist himself. Like so many Americans of the day, the team then got stuck into a groove and the next record, *My Baby Loves To Dance,* sounded too similar for comfort to its two predecessors and failed to sell in significant numbers. Montez continued to tour regularly and thus maintained a high profile despite the lack of hit records. In 1966, he re-surfaced as a recording artist on A & M Records with a much more laid back style to his earlier rock days. He just missed the U.K. charts on his A & M debut with his version of the much-recorded Tony Hatch song *Call Me* (he competed with a raucous version of the song by Lulu which also missed out on chart honours) but made the breakthrough in a big way with the next single, the Latin American sounding *The More I See You.* The follow-up *There Will Never Be Another You* again cloned its predecessor in delivery and was only a minor hit. With the hits long gone, Montez became a rare visitor to these shores although *Let's Dance* did chart on a re-release in 1972.

> **BIGGEST 1962 HIT : *Let's Dance.***
>
> **OTHER 60's CHART HITS INCLUDED :**
> ***Some Kinda Fun, The More I See You, There Will Never Be Another You.***

*I Remember You* **topped the charts for seven weeks during 1962. The record was the first of six top ten hits, including four number ones, for FRANK IFIELD.**

The Wearside Top Ten of mid August 1962 included three singles with a comedy theme. These were *Speedy Gonzales* (Pat Boone), *Come Outside* (Mike Sarne) and *Right Said Fred* (Bernard Cribbins).

Frank Ifield's *I Remember You* became the region's best selling single during the summer of 1962.

Buddy Holly-influenced Tommy Roe made his chart debut with *Sheila.*

Carole King and her babysitter Little Eva were simultaneously in the top three charts with *It Might As Well Rain Until September* and *The Locomotion* respectively. Both were Carole King penned songs.

Roger Miller made his chart debut as a songwriter when Del Shannon took *Swiss Maid* into the top ten. Miller charted as a singer some three years later with *King Of The Road.*

*Return To Sender* gave Elvis Presley the Christmas number one record.

Pat Boone had his twelfth and last top ten hit with *Speedy Gonzales.*

After several years of trying, Ronnie Carroll finally secured a top ten hit with his cover version of Bobby Vinton's U.S. smash *Roses Are Red.*

Ray Charles hit top spot for the only time in his distinguished chart career with *I Can't Stop Loving You.*

Tchaikovsky made his chart debut as a composer when his Nutcracker Suite, in somewhat modified form, was revived by B. Bumble & The Stingers as *Nut Rocker.*

As well as topping the U.K. charts in October, *Telstar* by The Tornados became the fastest ever selling British record in America.

# BRENDA LEE

Little Miss Dynamite was aptly named. Standing at just 4 feet 11 inches, fifteen year old Brenda Lee first cracked the British hit parade at the start of the decade with *Sweet Nothin's*. The song demanded a powerful vocal interpretation and the fact that she coped with ease belied that fact that such a strong voice could emanate from a child of such diminutive build. Lee's run of chart hits lasted exactly five years during which time she always lived up to her Little Miss Dynamite billing with a dynamic stage presence which put many of her more experienced fellow professionals to shame. Lee's roots were in country music but it was in mainstream pop that she found fame and fortune, alternating between rockers and ballads with apparent ease. Brenda Lee was a one-label chart artist, staying with Decca Records in America (which was released on the Brunswick label over here) for her entire chart career. Her hottest period was April 1962 - March 1963 when she scored with five hits on the Wearside charts. By 1964 the British beat invasion was well underway and Brenda Lee, shrewdly aware of the prevailing trends, began recording in the U.K. with in-vogue record producer Mickie Most who at that time was enjoying considerable success with The Animals and Herman's Hermits. The first fruits of the relationship was *Is It True* which was rush released in 1964. The following year was the last in which Brenda Lee's name was listed on the best selling singles charts. Family commitments reduced her touring drastically and with fewer live appearances it was always going to be an uphill struggle to compete with the new generation of pop. She later re-surfaced on the touring circuit in her original persona of a country artiste.

> **BIGGEST 1962 HIT : Speak To Me Pretty.**
>
> **OTHER 60's CHART HITS INCLUDED :**
> *Sweet Nothin's, Here Comes That Feeling, Rockin' Around The Christmas Tree, All Alone Am I, Losing You, As Usual.*

*ABOVE*
**THE BEATLES whose first Parlophone single *Love Me Do* was released on 4th October 1962.**

*RIGHT*
**BRENDA LEE with Jimmy Savile at the studios of Radio Luxembourg in 1962.**

## Wearside Top Ten ~ 13th February 1962

1. *The Young Ones* ... Cliff Richard & The Shadows (Columbia)
2. *Rock A Hula Baby/Can't Help Falling In Love* ....................... Elvis Presley (RCA)
3. *Let's Twist Again* ....................... Chubby Checker (Columbia)
4. *Forget Me Not* ......................... Eden Kane (Decca)
5. *Walk On By* ................................. Leroy Van Dyke (Mercury)
6. *Cryin' In The Rain* ......... The Everly Brothers (Warner Bros.)
7. *Happy Birthday Sweet Sixteen* ................ Neil Sedaka (RCA)
8. *I'd Never Find Another You* ...................... Billy Fury (Decca)
9. *Stranger On The Shore* ............... Mr. Acker Bilk (Columbia)
10. *Multiplication* ..................................... Bobby Darin (London)

## Wearside Top Ten ~ 24th April 1962

1. *Wonderful Land* ............................. The Shadows (Columbia)
2. *Dream Baby* ........................................ Roy Orbison (London)
3. *Hey Baby* ........................................ Bruce Channel (Mercury)
4. *When My Little Girl Is Smiling* ............. Jimmy Justice (Pye)
5. *Twistin' The Night Away* ........................... Sam Cooke (RCA)
6. *Speak To Me Pretty* .......................... Brenda Lee (Brunswick)
7. *Hey Little Girl* .................................... Del Shannon (London)
8. *Tell Me What He Said* .................. Helen Shapiro (Columbia)
9. *Rock A Hula Baby/Can't Help Falling In Love* ...................... Elvis Presley (RCA)
10. *Hole In The Ground* ............. Bernard Cribbins (Parlophone)

## Wearside Top Ten ~ 26th June 1962

1. *Come Outside* ................................ Mike Sarne (Parlophone)
2. *A Picture Of You* ................................ Joe Brown (Piccadilly)
3. *Ginny Come Lately* ............................. Brian Hyland (HMV)
4. *Good Luck Charm* ................................ Elvis Presley (RCA)
5. *Last Night Was Made For Love* ................ Billy Fury (Decca)
6. *I'm Looking Out The Window* ........ Cliff Richard (Columbia)
7. *I Can't Stop Loving You* ........................ Ray Charles (HMV)
8. *Nut Rocker* ............... B. Bumble & The Stingers (Top Rank)
9. *I Don't Know Why* ................................ Eden Kane (Decca)
10. *As You Like It* ................................ Adam Faith (Parlophone)

## Wearside Top Ten ~ 4th September 1962

1. *I Remember You* ................................ Frank Ifield (Columbia)
2. *Things* ................................ Bobby Darin (London)
3. *Roses Are Red* ................................ Ronnie Carroll (Philips)
4. *Speedy Gonzales* ................................ Pat Boone (London)
5. *Breaking Up Is Hard To Do* ................... Neil Sedaka (RCA)
6. *Sealed With A Kiss* ............................. Brian Hyland (HMV)
7. *She's Not You* ................................ Elvis Presley (RCA)
8. *Once Upon A Dream* ............................... Billy Fury (Decca)
9. *Guitar Tango* ................................ The Shadows (Columbia)
10. *Vacation* ................................ Connie Francis (MGM)

## THE FOUR SEASONS

The Four Seasons comprised Frankie Valli, Bob Gaudio, Mick Massi and Tommy Devito. The nucleus of the group existed in many guises from 1953 until they eventually hit the big time in 1962. The outfit had a highly distinctive sound of falsetto harmony pop which was largely reliant upon Valli's vocals and Bob Crewe's razor sharp productions. The Four Seasons made their U.K. chart debut in October 1962, exactly one week ahead of The Beatles and in the fashion conscious world of popular music, that fact alone allowed them to ride the storm which capsized many of their fellow Americans in the stormy waters of the British beat boom. They had seven chart hits in this country but were never able to repeat their mammoth run of chart successes in America where their infallibility was such that their record label released a *Battle Of The Bands* album featuring The Seasons and The Beatles at the height of the Liverpudlians' popularity in 1964. Two of the group's American hits which hardly saw the light of day in Britain, *Bye Bye Baby* and *Working My Way Back To You*, were subsequently covered by Bay City Rollers (in 1975) and Detroit Spinners (in 1980) and both became number one hits. After several months without a major U.K. hit, The Four Seasons bounced back in fine style with the wistful *Rag Doll* during the summer of 1964. The flip-side of the record, *Silence Is Golden*, was successfully covered by The Tremeloes in 1967 and gave the British band their only chart topper. The group were not a major touring outfit during the sixties, instead relying upon their inspired studio recordings and the productions of Bob Crewe to stabilise their popularity. Although regarded as a sixties group, The Four Seasons eclipsed their early successes in the mid seventies with a run of hits which included a U.K. number one, *December '63 (Oh What A Night)*.

**BIGGEST 1962 HIT : Sherry.**

**OTHER 60's CHART HITS INCLUDED :**
*Big Girls Don't Cry, Walk Like A Man, Rag Doll, Let's Hang On, I've Got You Under My Skin, Opus 17 (Don't You Worry 'Bout Me).*

*The Party's Over* proved to be just that for Lonnie Donegan as it was to be his final top ten hit.

Bruce Channel's *Hey Baby* hit featured harmonica playing which influenced two of the year's subsequent hits; *I Remember You* (Frank Ifield) and *Love Me Do* (The Beatles).

The aforementioned *Nut Rocker* by B. Bumble & The Stingers displaced *Wonderful Land* by The Shadows from the number one spot. This statistic created pop history as it was the first occasion that one instrumental had displaced another from the chart's summit.

**RAY CHARLES**
**who topped the charts in 1962 with**
*I Can't Stop Loving You.*

22

# JOE MEEK

Quite simply, Joe Meek was the most innovative British record producer in the history of popular music. The self-styled, inventive producer worked from a flat above a shop in Holloway Road, North London from where he employed a variety of unconventional methods to obtain unique sound effects on his records. The methods often involved the use of a domestic reel to reel tape recorder and using this he would gleefully pit his wits against the in-house producers of the big record companies with their state of the art equipment. Once recorded, Meek leased his tapes to the likes of EMI, Decca, and Pye via his company RGM Sound. His work, which invariably made liberal use of echo, was dismissed by some sections of the music industry as being gimmicky and novel but such insulting accusations merely drove him on to greater successes. Meek's introduction to the record industry was in 1954 when he joined IBC as a recording engineer and subsequently worked on hits by Lonnie Donegan, Frankie Vaughan and Johnny Duncan. As a producer his first hit was *Angela Jones* by Michael Cox on his own short-lived Triumph label. There then followed a veritable plethora of chart hits with John Leyton (*Johnny Remember Me*), The Tornados (*Telstar*) and The Honeycombs (*Have I The Right*) all benefitting from Joe Meek inspired chart toppers. Undoubtedly, his golden period was 1960-1965 but as the decade progressed his increasingly eccentric and erratic behaviour alienated him to record company personnel. Meek's tempestuous personality and mental instability finally culminated in a bizarre shooting incident in which he fatally shot first his landlady and then himself. The date, 3rd January 1967, marked the eighth anniversary of the death of Buddy Holly, Joe Meek's idol.

> ***BIGGEST 1962 HIT : Telstar (The Tornados).***
>
> ***OTHER 60's CHART HITS INCLUDED :***
> ***Angela Jones (Michael Cox), Johnny Remember Me, Wild Wind (John Leyton), Tribute To Buddy Holly,***
> ***Don't You Think It's Time (Mike Berry), Globetrotter (The Tornados), Just Like Eddie (Heinz), Have I The Right,***
> ***That's The Way (The Honeycombs).***

## *Wearside Top Ten ~ 30th October 1962*

1. *Telstar* .................................................. The Tornados (Decca)
2. *The Locomotion* ...................................... Little Eva (London)
3. *Sheila* ...................................................... Tommy Roe (HMV)
4. *Let's Dance* ........................................ Chris Montez (London)
5. *It Might As Well Rain Until September* .....................................
   Carole King (London)
6. *Venus In Blue Jeans* ................................ Mark Wynter (Pye)
7. *Swiss Maid* ........................................ Del Shannon (London)
8. *Ramblin' Rose* .............................. Nat 'King' Cole (Capitol)
9. *Sherry* ........................................ The Four Seasons (Stateside)
10. *She's Not You* .......................................... Elvis Presley (RCA)

## *Wearside Top Ten ~ 27th December 1962*

1. *Return To Sender* .................................. Elvis Presley (RCA)
2. *The Next Time* ................................ Cliff Richard (Columbia)
3. *Dance On* ...................................... The Shadows (Columbia)
4. *(Dance With) The Guitar Man* .............. Duane Eddy (RCA)
5. *Rockin' Around The Christmas Tree* .....................................
   Brenda Lee (Brunswick)
6. *Sun Arise* ............................................ Rolf Harris (Columbia)
7. *Lovesick Blues* ................................ Frank Ifield (Columbia)
8. *Bobby's Girl* .................................. Susan Maughan (Philips)
9. *Desafinado* ...................... Stan Getz & Charlie Byrd (HMV)
10. *Your Cheating Heart* .......................... Ray Charles (HMV)

**PAT BOONE**
**whose impressive chart run came to an end**
**in 1962 with *The Main Attraction*.**

In 1962 two major touring shows visited the Odeon Cinema in Sunderland. The first, on 8th March, was 'The Big Star Show of 1962' which starred Billy Fury, John Leyton, Eden Kane, Karl Denver and Joe Brown.

Later in the year, on 13th November, the same venue played host to a touring package featuring Billy Fury, Karl Denver, Joe Brown, Mike Sarne, Marty Wilde, Jimmy Justice and Mark Wynter.

# BILLY FURY

Ronald Wycherley - alias Billy Fury - was Britain's first truly great Rock & Roll singer. He was a singer's singer, widely acknowledged by his fellow artists as being their role model. Wycherley was born in Liverpool in 1940 and recorded his first chart hit in 1959, four years before the term 'Merseybeat' was first coined. Billy Fury was Decca Records' most successful recording artist of all time with some twenty six chart hits spanning the period 1959 to 1966. His first love was Rock & Roll but Decca recognised his potential as a balladeer of teen love songs and provided him with a seemingly endless supply of such material to enhance his obvious sex appeal. Fury was one of the leading concert performers of the early sixties with a carefully selected stage repertoire which showcased the full extent of his musical capabilities; an opportunity denied to him by his record company. Incredibly, he never experienced the thrill of a number one record, stalling at number two with *Jealousy* in 1961 and peaking at number three on three other occasions. His chart run extended well into the beat group era and this was largely due to the fact that on stage, backed firstly by The Tornados and then The Gamblers, he could rock with the best of them and with as much contemporary style as his modern day chart rivals. Fury's survival as a major chart name, and a balladeer at that, was surpassed only by Cliff Richard from the old school of pop stars but came to an end with the hit *Give Me Your Word* in September 1966. Throughout his career, Billy Fury had been the victim of recurring heart problems and it was to be ill health which curtailed his showbiz activities for much of the seventies. In 1981, his career was re-activated after he signed with Polydor Records. After three minor hits, Billy Fury died of heart failure on 28th January 1983. Almost uniquely, Billy Fury's reputation has grown over the years and his name is held in even higher regard today than it was in his halcyon hit parade days.

> **BIGGEST 1962 HIT : *Last Night Was Made For Love.***
>
> **OTHER 60's CHART HITS INCLUDED :**
> *Halfway To Paradise, I'd Never Find Another You, Once Upon A Dream, Like I've Never Been Gone, When Will You Say I Love You, In Summer, In Thoughts Of You.*

The first steps were taken to provide Wearsiders with late licence cabaret entertainment when a late drink licence was granted to the Vine Grill in Albion Place. The Sunderland Echo reported that this move would 'ensure that Sunderland could now offer the facilities which are commonplace down south'. Although an application by nearby Wetherells for a music, singing and dancing licence was rejected in September, it would only be a matter of time before they and a host of other nightspots were granted the necessary licences to transform the face of north east nightlife.

# *The Ones That Got Away In ...*

| | |
|---|---|
| *Norman* | Carol Deene |
| *Please Don't Ask About Barbara* | Bobby Vee |
| *It Keeps Right On A Hurtin'* | Johnny Tillotson |
| *Keep Away From Other Girls* | Helen Shapiro |
| *Susie Darlin'* | Tommy Roe |
| *He's Old Enough To Know Better* | The Brook Brothers |
| *House To Let* | Eden Kane |
| *Big Man* | Kathy Kirby |
| *I'm Gonna Be Warm This Winter* | Connie Francis |
| *Chains* | The Cookies |

Carol Deene became the centre of some fun poking when her releases were regularly criticised on television's Juke Box Jury after which it was invariably revealed that she was the programme's surprise backstage guest who subsequently came out to face the panel. *Norman* was one of four catchy records from the early sixties which should have put Carol Deene's name into the top ten.

All American boys Bobby Vee, Johnny Tillotson and Tommy Roe struggled chartwise with their respective releases as their recording techniques were showing early signs of becoming passé with British record buyers.

*Chains* by The Cookies impressed The Beatles so much that they included the song on their debut LP. Although The Cookies' recording was a major hit in their native America, it scraped into the British charts at number fifty for just one week.

# In 1963 ...

*Like I Do* by Maureen Evans gave the tiny independent Oriole record label its only top ten hit of the decade.

*Dance On* by The Shadows was displaced from the number one spot by ex Shadows Jet Harris & Tony Meehan and their recording of *Diamonds.*

The first week of February saw The Beatles in the region's top ten charts for the first time. The record was *Please Please Me.*

LEFT
**This 1963 advertisement from a pop concert programme is a flash-back to the type of value for money shows which were on offer during the early to mid sixties.**

RIGHT
**An early photograph of ROY ORBISON who made the top ten with *In Dreams, Falling* and *Blue Bayou* during 1963.**

Frank Ifield's *Wayward Wind* hit top spot on the chart and gave him a hat-trick of number ones, following on from *I Remember You* and *Lovesick Blues.*

After a run of twenty three consecutive top ten hits, Elvis Presley failed to make the top ten with *One Broken Heart For Sale.*

## GERRY & THE PACEMAKERS

One of several acts to be managed by Brian Epstein during the sixties (others included The Beatles, Billy J. Kramer & The Dakotas, The Fourmost and Cilla Black), Gerry & The Pacemakers comprised Gerry Marsden, Freddie Marsden, Les Chadwick and Les Maguire. The group was spotted by EMI's George Martin in November 1962 and immediately offered a recording contract with the company's Columbia label. Gerry & The Pacemakers' first recording session in January 1963 produced three cuts including *How Do You Do It* which had earlier been rejected by The Beatles. The Mitch Murray penned song was released as the group's debut single and catapulted to pole position, selling over 500,000 copies in the process. The follow-up single, another Mitch Murray composition, *I Like It,* repeated the achievement of its predecessor while a change in musical direction produced the group's third and most successful release *You'll Never Walk Alone* (from Carousel) which sold 776,000 copies to become Gerry & The Pacemakers' biggest U.K. hit and also their third number one. The success gave the group the unique distinction (finally equalled twenty one years later by Frankie Goes To Hollywood) of having number one hit singles with their first three releases. The group's debut LP *How Do You Like It* became a best seller while Gerry's cheeky persona was well received in America where the hit singles came thick and fast during 1964-1966. After two years of almost uninterrupted U.K. chart success, the group's record sales suffered a marked decline in 1965 as tastes began to move away from the Merseybeat style of pop. *Ferry 'Cross The Mersey* from the film of the same name gave Gerry & The Pacemakers their last top ten hit during the early weeks of the year and although minor hits followed, 1965 was to be the group's final year of chart action. With rock music nudging the Mersey sound out of the spotlight, the group split up in 1966 at which point Marsden spent the remainder of the decade seeking solace as a solo artist on the cabaret circuit.

> **BIGGEST 1963 HIT : *You'll Never Walk Alone.***
>
> **OTHER 60's CHART HITS INCLUDED :**
> *How Do You Do It, I Like It, I'm The One, Don't Let The Sun Catch You Crying, Ferry 'Cross The Mersey.*

# BILLY J. KRAMER & THE DAKOTAS

Billy J. Kramer (real name William Howard Ashton) was spotted by Brian Epstein at Liverpool's Cavern Club in 1962. At the time, Kramer was singing with Liverpool group The Coasters who turned down the chance to sign with Epstein's NEMS company as full time professionals. Kramer did leave his day job with British Railways and was teamed with Manchester group The Dakotas. In March 1963 Billy J. Kramer & The Dakotas signed a recording deal with Parlophone and soon began recording with George Martin. Thanks to the Brian Epstein connection the group had access to Lennon-McCartney songs and chose *Do You Want To Know A Secret* (which at that time had just been recorded by The Beatles for their forthcoming *Please Please Me* LP) for their first single. It proved to be an inspired choice as the record climbed to number two on the hit parade and became the first of four Lennon-McCartney songs to be successfully covered by Billy J. Kramer & The Dakotas. The group's biggest chart hit - not a Beatles number - was *Little Children* which became a worldwide million seller in 1964. The song topped the Wearside chart for three weeks and was reportedly released against the advice of Epstein. After a meteoric rise to stardom, Kramer's career was beginning to show signs of struggle by 1965. After a flop single, he turned to the songwriting talents of Burt Bacharach & Hal David to restore his chart glory with *Trains And Boats And Planes* which, despite spending one week on the Wearside top ten, lost out to Bacharach's own version of the song in the race for major chart honours. Thereafter it was downhill all the way for Kramer's recording career. These were times of rapidly changing fashions in popular music and the group appeared to be unwilling - or unable - to break away from the sounds of the fading Merseyside beat boom. Kramer and The Dakotas split in 1968 and the former continued his career as a solo performer on the club circuit.

> *BIGGEST 1963 HIT : Bad To Me.*
>
> *OTHER 60's CHART HITS INCLUDED :*
> *Do You Want To Know A Secret, I'll Keep You Satisfied, From A Window, Little Children,*
> *Trains And Boats And Planes.*

*Do You Want To Know A Secret* by Billy J. Kramer & The Dakotas became the first cover version of a Lennon McCartney song to hit the charts.

The first four records in the top ten in mid-June all featured Liverpool acts. The records were *From Me To You* (The Beatles), *Do You Want To Know A Secret* (Billy J. Kramer & The Dakotas), *When Will You Say I Love You* (Billy Fury) and *I Like It* (Gerry & The Pacemakers).

Japanese Kyu Sakamoto hit the region's top ten charts with *Sukiyaki*.

The first national hit by The Rolling Stones, *Come On,* failed to dent any of the regional charts.

The Caravelles had their one and only top ten sixties hit with the distinctive *You Don't Have To Be A Baby To Cry.*

### Wearside Top Ten ~ 21st February 1963

1. *The Wayward Wind* ............................ Frank Ifield (Columbia)
2. *Please Please Me* ........................... The Beatles (Parlophone)
3. *Diamonds* ....................... Jet Harris & Tony Meehan (Decca)
4. *The Night Has A Thousand Eyes* .......... Bobby Vee (Liberty)
5. *Little Town Flirt* ................................ Del Shannon (London)
6. *Loop-De-Loop* ............................. Frankie Vaughan (Philips)
7. *Island Of Dreams* .......................... The Springfields (Philips)
8. *Walk Right In* ........................ The Rooftop Singers (Fontana)
9. *That's What Love Will Do* ................. Joe Brown (Piccadilly)
10. *Don't You Think It's Time* ....................... Mike Berry (HMV)

### Wearside Top Ten ~ 18th April 1963

1. *How Do You Do It* ...... Gerry & The Pacemakers (Columbia)
2. *From A Jack To A King* ........................ Ned Miller (London)
3. *Brown Eyed Handsome Man* ................ Buddy Holly (Coral)
4. *The Folk Singer* ..................................... Tommy Roe (HMV)
5. *Rhythm Of The Rain* ................ The Cascades (Warner Bros.)
6. *Say Wonderful Things* ...................... Ronnie Carroll (Philips)
7. *Like I've Never Been Gone* ...................... Billy Fury (Decca)
8. *In Dreams* ........................................ Roy Orbison (London)
9. *Say I Won't Be There* ................... The Springfields (Philips)
10. *Summer Holiday* ............................. Cliff Richard (Columbia)

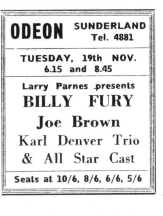

The late great BILLY FURY topping
the bill in Sunderland during 1963
as did JOE BROWN during
the same year.

The Beatles' *Twist And Shout* EP hit the singles charts; a feat almost unheard of. At the time, an EP cost 11/5d (57p) compared with 6/8d (33p) for a single. The Beatles' EP even had to compete with a single version of the song by Brian Poole & The Tremeloes.

Towards the end of the year, Gerry & The Pacemakers became the first sixties recording stars to hit top spot with their first three single releases. They did it with *How Do You Do It*, *I Like It* and *You'll Never Walk Alone*.

In the final chart before Christmas, The Beatles displaced themselves from the number one spot when *I Want To Hold Your Hand* took over at the top from *She Loves You* and remained at number one throughout the region well into the new year.

'Coronation Street' actor Chris Sandford became the first soap star to hit the regional charts when *Not Too Little Not Too Much* just scraped into the lower reaches of the best sellers.

*Charmaine* gave The Bachelors their first of eight top ten hits in a Decca chart career which spanned three years.

Two singers with the surname Berry hit the charts with *Memphis Tennessee*. Surprisingly, it was one of only two top ten hits for Chuck Berry in the sixties while the song launched the recording career of Dave Berry who went on to score further hits with *The Crying Game* (1964), *Little Things* (1965) and *Mama* (1966).

The first Adam Faith record to miss the top twenty since he hit the big time was the wistful *Baby Take A Bow*.

## RAY CHARLES

Few recording artists genuinely deserve the accolade 'genius'. Ray Charles is one of the exceptions. His recording career has spanned over forty years during which time he has excelled as vocalist, composer, pianist and producer. His music defies catergorizing with a talent which comfortably embraces Gospel, Jazz, Country and even Popular/MOR. Charles was born in Georgie, U.S.A. on 23rd September 1930 into extreme poverty. He was blind by the age of seven as a result of glaucoma and was orphaned shortly after his fifteenth birthday. He learned to read - and later to write - music in braille and developed his talent for playing a variety of musical instruments, notably the piano. Using Nat 'King' Cole as an early role model, he began working as a vocalist/pianist at local nightclubs. In 1952 he secured a recording contract with Atlantic Records for whom he made a string of critically acclaimed records. However, it was not until he left the label for ABC Records (leased to HMV in this country) that he found musical and commercial freedom. He then unleashed a succession of breathtakingly exuberant singles on to an unsuspecting British public who hailed him as a superstar almost overnight. His unpredictable musical direction as he moved from one release to another further enhanced his stature as one of the all-time greats. Ironically, the downslide as a recording artist came when he began recording Beatles' songs towards the latter part of the decade. His interpretations of *Yesterday* and *Eleanor Rigby* seemed to be one step too far along the road of diversification for the comfort of his fans and the hits dried up although Ray Charles has remained a major albums artist into the nineties.

> **BIGGEST 1963 HIT : *Take These Chains From My Heart*.**
>
> **OTHER 60's CHART HITS INCLUDED :**
> *Hit The Road Jack, I Can't Stop Loving You, You Don't Know Me, Your Cheating Heart, Georgia On My Mind.*

Buddy Holly's posthumous releases cracked the top ten three times during the year; *Brown Eyed Handsome Man*, *Bo Diddley* and *Wishing* all kept the U.S. flag flying in a year which was dominated by British beat groups.

The Beatles were frequent visitors to the north east. They played at Majestic Ballroom, Newcastle (January and June), Rink Ballroom, Sunderland (May) and Astoria Ballroom, Middlesbrough (June). Higher profile shows included a British tour where they supported Helen Shapiro and appeared alongside Danny Williams, Kenny Lynch, The Kestrels and The Red Price Band. The first leg of the tour closed at the Empire Theatre, Sunderland on 9th February. The second leg resumed on 23rd February and during the interim the group recorded ten of the tracks for their debut *Please Please Me* LP. Included in The Kestrels' line up was one Tony Burrows who subsequently found top ten chart fame with Edison Lighthouse and White Plains.

*RIGHT*
**THE DAKOTAS'** main claim to fame was as backing group to Billy J. Kramer although they had a brief moment of chart glory themselves with *The Cruel Sea* in 1963.

*BELOW*
**THE FOURMOST** whose chart debut in 1963 was with Lennon & McCartney's *Hello Little Girl.*

THE DAKOTAS

THE FOURMOST

The Beatles subsequently played on a 21 date tour with Tommy Roe, Chris Montez and The Viscounts which visited City Hall, Newcastle on 23rd March. By the time of the north east show, The Beatles had been promoted from third act on the bill (from a line up of seven attractions) to top of the bill.

A relentless touring schedule by The Beatles saw visits to Globe Cinema, Stockton (22nd November), City Hall Newcastle (23rd November) and Empire Theatre, Sunderland (30th November).

The "Your Lucky Stars" touring package visited Sunderland's Odeon Cinema on 27th February and starred no fewer than seven chart acts of the day in Joe Brown, The Tornados, Susan Maughan, Jess Conrad, Eden Kane Rolf Harris and Shane Fenton.

## THE BEATLES

Quite simply, a pop music phenomenon. The Beatles' achievements as the greatest popular music group the world has ever seen will, in all probability, never be equalled. The Beatles name was born in April 1960 and originally comprised John Lennon, Paul McCartney, George Harrison, Pete Best and Stuart Sutcliffe. In March 1961 the group made their debut at Liverpool's Cavern Club and followed this with a trip to Hamburg lasting three months. By early 1962, Sutcliffe had left the group (he died shortly afterwards), Brian Epstein had become manager and a recording audition with Decca Records had ended in failure. The Beatles were signed to EMI's Parlophone label by George Martin in July 1962 and soon afterwards Pete Best was sacked and Ringo Starr became a Beatle. The group's first single, *Love Me Do*, became a minor hit in late 1962 but nobody could have forecast the success story that was waiting just around the corner. *Please Please Me* gave the group their first top ten hit in January 1963 while the follow-up *From Me To You* became the first of eleven consecutive number ones and the first of seventeen number ones in total. The Beatles toured the length and breadth of Britain and their singles, EPs and LPs sold in unprecedented quantities. Beatlemania hit America in January 1964 when *I Want To Hold Your Hand* became their first major Stateside release and soared to the top of the charts. Within three months, The Beatles occupied all top five positions in the U.S. chart; the record business would never be the same again! Beatles' songs provided a rich source of material for numerous chart groups of the day including Billy J. Kramer & The Dakotas, The Fourmost and The Overlanders while the group themselves scored further successes with their films *A Hard Day's Night* and *Help!* in 1964 and 1965 respectively. By 1967, the group announced that their touring days were over. Meanwhile EMI revealed that total world sales of Beatles' records had topped 200 million. The group moved comfortably into the psychedelic era during the so-called 'Summer Of Love' with what many regarded as their finest moment; the *Sergeant Pepper's Lonely Hearts Club Band* LP. The hits continued to come thick and fast throughout the late sixties but, by then, cracks were beginning to appear in the musical and personal relationships of John, Paul, George and Ringo. An era which The Beatles helped to create in 1963 came to an end in 1970 when the group was finally and acrimoniously dissolved.

*BIGGEST 1963 HIT : She Loves You.*

*OTHER 60's CHART HITS INCLUDED :*
*I Want To Hold Your Hand, Can't Buy Me Love, I Feel Fine, Ticket To Ride, Day Tripper, All You Need Is Love,*
*Hello Goodbye, Hey Jude, Get Back.*

## Wearside Top Ten ~ 20th June 1963

1. *From Me To You* ............................. The Beatles (Parlophone)
2. *I Like It* ....................... Gerry & The Pacemakers (Columbia)
3. *Do You Want To Know A Secret* ..................................................
Billy J. Kramer & The Dakotas (Parlophone)
4. *If You Gotta Make A Fool Of Somebody* .........................
Freddie & The Dreamers (Columbia)
5. *Deck Of Cards* ............................. Wink Martindale (London)
6. *When Will You Say I Love You* ................... Billy Fury (Decca)
7. *Take These Chains From My Heart* ....... Ray Charles (HMV)
8. *Falling* ................................................. Roy Orbison (London)
9. *Forget Him* ......................... Bobby Rydell (Cameo-Parkway)
10. *Young Lovers* ....................................... Paul & Paula (Philips)

## Wearside Top Ten ~ 22nd August 1963

1. *Sweets For My Sweet* ............................. The Searchers (Pye)
2. *Bad To Me* ....... Billy J. Kramer & The Dakotas (Parlophone)
3. *I'm Telling You Now* .... Freddie & The Dreamers (Columbia)
4. *In Summer* ................................................... Billy Fury (Decca)
5. *Confessin'* ..................................................... Frank Ifield (Columbia)
6. *Da Doo Ron Ron* ................................. The Crystals (London)
7. *Twist And Shout* ........ Brian Poole & The Tremeloes (Decca)
8. *Wipe Out* ................................................... The Surfaris (London)
9. *You Don't Have To Be A Baby To Cry* ...............................
The Caravelles (Decca)
10. *I'll Never Get Over You* ..............................................................
Johnny Kidd & The Pirates (HMV)

# FRANK IFIELD

1963 was a watershed in popular music. The British beat groups arrived en masse and brought about unparalleled changes to the record industry. For the over thirties who struggled to come to terms with the new sounds emanating from Liverpool et al, Frank Ifield was the perfect antidote. Ifield was born in Coventry in 1936 and at the age of nine emigrated with his family to Australia. He returned to England in 1959 and within a year had his first taste of chart success with *Lucky Devil*. The big breakthrough came in 1962 when the harmonica laden *I Remember You* soared to the top of the Wearside chart and became the first record to sell over one million copies in Britain. By February 1963, Ifield wrote pop history when he became the first artist to score three consecutive number one records on the British charts after *Lovesick Blues* and *The Wayward Wind* matched the feat of the aforementioned *I Remember You*. By now, Frank Ifield's extraordinary yodelling ability had become his trademark and helped pave the way for a further three hits including another chart topper. Frank's affinity for Country and Western music was apparent on most of his chart hits and his laid back vocal style endeared him to a distinct section of the record buying public. His demise as a major recording name was as sudden as it was unexpected. Unlike the fall from grace suffered by the early sixties American teen idols, Frank Ifield's dwindling record sales from 1964 onwards could hardly be blamed upon the domination of Beatlemania and its spin-offs, as the two sounds appealed to distinctly different areas of the market. The newer material was not significantly weaker than the 1962/1963 recordings but, nevertheless, the notoriously fickle nature of the record buying public had condemned Frank to pantomime work and the supper club circuit by 1967.

**BIGGEST 1963 HIT : *The Wayward Wind.***

**OTHER 60's CHART HITS INCLUDED :**
***I Remember You, Lovesick Blues, Nobody's Darlin' But Mine, Confessin', Don't Blame Me.***

## Wearside Top Ten ~ 31st October 1963

1. *Do You Love Me* ....... Brian Poole & The Tremeloes (Decca)
2. *She Loves You* ...................................... The Beatles (Parlophone)
3. *You'll Never Walk Alone* ..........................................................
Gerry & The Pacemakers (Columbia)
4. *Blue Bayou* ............................................... Roy Orbison (London)
5. *Then He Kissed Me* ........................... The Crystals (London)
6. *Sugar And Spice* ....................................... The Searchers (Pye)
7. *Be My Baby* ............................................... The Ronettes (London)
8. *Hello Little Girl* ..................................... The Fourmost (Parlophone)
9. *The First Time* ....................................... Adam Faith (Parlophone)
10. *Everybody* ................................................... Tommy Roe (HMV)

## Wearside Top Ten ~ 19th December 1963

1. *I Want To Hold Your Hand* ............. The Beatles (Parlophone)
2. *She Loves You* ................................. The Beatles (Parlophone)
3. *Glad All Over* ..................... The Dave Clark Five (Columbia)
4. *Secret Love* ........................................... Kathy Kirby (Decca)
5. *You Were Made For Me* ...........................................................
Freddie & The Dreamers (Columbia)
6. *Maria Elena* ............................. Los Indios Tabajaras (RCA)
7. *I Only Want To Be With You* ........ Dusty Springfield (Philips)
8. *Twenty Four Hours From Tulsa* .........................................
Gene Pitney (United Artists)
9. *Swinging On A Star* .......................... Big Dee Irwin (Colpix)
10. *Money* ........................... Bern Elliott & The Fenmen (Decca)

RIGHT
THE CRYSTALS who teamed up with ace record producer Phil Spector to score with two of the year's most memorable hits, *Da Doo Ron Ron* and *Then He Kissed Me*.

Further pop concerts to be staged in Sunderland included a package starring John Leyton/Gene Vincent/Jet Harris & Tony Meehan at the Odeon on 30th March, Adam Faith at the Sunderland Empire for one week from 27th May, Eden Kane at Seaburn Hall on 1st June and Cliff Bennett & The Rebel Rousers at Seaburn Hall on 20th July.

21st March saw the official opening of Wetherells Club by television and recording star Ronnie Hilton. The club advertised itself as a Wining/Dining/Dancing/Gaming/Cabaret venue with two cocktail bars and boasted an extended drinks licence until 2.00a.m. on a Friday, Saturday and Monday. Such late drinking hours were virtually unheard of outside of London in those days and the owners said that it was their aim to make Wetherells into the finest nightspot in Northern England. Membership to the club cost one guinea.

# PHIL SPECTOR

Phil Spector's music was nothing at all like that of Joe Meek. Both record producers did, however, share a number of traits. Both were independent insomuch that they were not tied to a particular record company, they were innovative, self-styled, eccentric to varying degrees and totally unconventional in their approach to making pop records. Harvey Phillip Spector was born in New York during 1940 and recorded his first million seller, *To Know Him Is To Love Him* by The Teddy Bears before his eighteenth birthday. He subsequently enjoyed notable successes as both composer (*Spanish Harlem*) and producer (Curtis Lee's *Pretty Little Angel Eyes*) before going on to create his much imitated Wall Of Sound in 1962. This involved an intense production technique which relied upon the most lavish orchestration ever heard on pop records at that time, layer upon layer of percussion and a veritable abundance of echo. The entire sound was recorded in glorious mono - Spector made a major issue of his dislike for stereo at that time - with The Ronettes, The Crystals, The Righteous Brothers and Ike & Tina Turner all benefitting from Spector's classic recordings of the era. In 1963, Phil Spector assembled his premier acts such as The Ronettes and The Crystals to perform a collection of seasonal favourites. The recordings were given the unmistakable Spector production treatment and released under the title *A Christmas Gift To You*. The set is now regarded as a classic with annual seasonal airings to this day. Most of Spector's releases featured the work of some of the best songwriters of the day with Goffin-King, Mann-Weil and Barry-Greenwich all contributing to his successes. When Spector's most ambitious project - *River Deep Mountain High* - was largely ignored by record buyers in his native America he took umbrage and unceremoniously retired from the music business in 1966. He subsequently re-surfaced in 1969 and became involved with The Beatles' *Let It Be* album as well as projects with both John Lennon and George Harrison.

*BIGGEST 1963 HIT : Be My Baby (The Ronettes).*

*OTHER 60's CHART HITS INCLUDED :*
*Baby I Love You (The Ronettes), Da Doo Ron Ron, Then He Kissed Me (The Crystals),*
*River Deep Mountain High (Ike & Tina Turner), You've Lost That Lovin' Feelin' (The Righteous Brothers).*

**THE SWINGING BLUE JEANS**
who first hit the big time with *Hippy Hippy Shake*.

The opening of Wetherells night club in March paved the way for a plethora of late night cabaret clubs in Sunderland. By late 1963, a licence had been granted for a 'continental style' night club to be opened above the Westminster Bank in Fawcett Street. The club opened as La Strada.

Gerry & The Pacemakers visited the Sunderland Empire for two houses of a one night stand on 2nd November. During the first performance, around thirty teenage girls rushed into the orchestra pit during the show and attempted to climb on to the stage. It took several policemen, doorkeepers and usherettes to return the screaming fans to their seats. Also on the bill that night were Del Shannon, Jet Harris & Tony Meehan, The Bachelors and chart debutant Cilla Black.

Other pop concerts in Sunderland during 1963 included John Leyton (10th September at The Rink), Danny Williams (week commencing 10th September at Wetherells), Johnny Kidd & The Pirates (6th October at Sunderland Empire), The Hollies and Shane Fenton & The Fentones (8th October at The Rink), The Casuals and The Connaughts (2nd November at Seaburn Hall), Lonnie Donegan (7th November at Sunderland Empire), Joe Brown, Billy Fury and Karl Denver (19th November at The Odeon).

# *The Ones That Got Away In ...*

| | |
|---|---|
| *I Saw Linda Yesterday* .......................... Doug Sheldon | *Cupboard Love* ................................... John Leyton |
| *Mr Bass Man* ...................................... Johnny Cymbal | *The Girl Sang The Blues* ...... The Everly Brothers |
| *Our Day Will Come* .............. Ruby & The Romantics | *Sugar Shack* ........ Jimmy Gilmer & The Fireballs |
| *Foolish Little Girl* ................................... The Shirelles | *Judy's Turn to Cry* ............................. Lesley Gore |
| *Blue Girl* .................................................. The Bruisers | *Busted* ................................................. Ray Charles |
| *Don't Do That* ............ Shane Fenton & The Fentones | *By The Way* ................................... The Big Three |
| *Don't Hang Up* .......................................... The Orlons | *My Boyfriend's Back* .......................... The Angels |
| *Five Hundred Miles Away From Home* ..... Bobby Bare | *I Can't Stay Mad At You* .................. Skeeter Davis |

With Americans suffering a major decline in chart fortunes, some excellent singles undeservedly fell by the wayside. *The Girl Sang The Blues* was The Everly Brothers' most underrated release of their recording career while Lesley Gore's *Judy's Turn To Cry* - sequel to *It's My Party* - would normally have been guaranteed a chart outing but was completely overlooked.

Likewise, the biggest non Beatles U.S. hit of the year was *Sugar Shack* which received relentless airplay over here, most notably on the Decca sponsored Radio Luxembourg Shows. Despite its heavy promotion, it failed to more than dent the charts, a fate which also befell American hits by Ruby & The Romantics, The Shirelles, The Orlons and The Angels.

One of the year's big surprise failures was The Bruisers' *Blue Girl*. Tommy Bruce's backing group released a beat record with all the in-vogue ingredients of a top five hit, but --- another time, another place.

# In 1964 ...

Decca recording stars The Applejacks made their chart debut with their only top ten hit *Tell Me When* and followed it with two minor hits, Lennon & McCartney's *Like Dreamers Do* and *Three Little Words*.

Louis Armstrong won the *Hello Dolly* race for chart honours when he registered a top five hit with the song, well ahead of cover versions by Frankie Vaughan and Kenny Ball.

The Barron Knights cracked the charts with the first of three comedy parodies when the double sided *Call Up The Groups* rose to number three.

The Beach Boys finally repeated their American successes in Britain when *I Get Around* gave them their chart debut. It was the first of ten top ten hits during the decade.

*House Of The Rising Sun* gave The Animals their only chart topper.

Doris Day had her only hit of the entire decade with *Move Over Darling*.

*I Only Want To Be With You* gave Dusty Springfield her first of ten top ten chart hits of the sixties.

Following her 1962 hit *The Locomotion*, Little Eva failed to seriously dent the charts with her two subsequent releases - *Keep Your Hands Off My Baby* and *Let's Turkey Trot* - but she struck it rich when she teamed up with Big Dee Irwin on *Swinging On A Star*.

The Rolling Stones hit top spot with *It's All Over Now*. It was the first of five consecutive number ones for the group.

As Jim Reeves' recording of *I Won't Forget You* climbed the charts, the singer was killed in an aeroplane crash.

There were U.K. chart toppers for two stalwarts of the American songwriting industry. The songs were th Goffin-King number *I'm Into Something Good* and Bacharach-David's *(There's) Always Something There T Remind Me*. The U.K. chart toppers were recorded by Herman's Hermits and Sandie Shaw respectively.

## ROY ORBISON

The 'Big O' became the most durable of all American solo performers in the wake of the Merseybeat chart onslaught circa 1963. He survived the ordeal with panache. Indeed, in mid 1964 he became the first American act to top the U.K. charts for eleven months when *It': Over* became Orbison's fastest selling record in three years. Five months later, he repeated the achievement with *Oh Pretty Woman*. Roy Orbison was born in Texas, U.S.A. in 1936 and during the early to mid sixties embarked upon an incredible run of mostly self-compose hit singles which invariably reflected upon the sombre side of life. His carefully cultivated image which saw him clad head to toe in black complimented his doom laden ballads of losers in love while the dark spectacles became the essential 'Big O' trademark. Sadly, his privat life was littered with tragedy and could almost be viewed as an enactment of the tales of lost love and despair contained within his songs In 1960, Orbison signed with the tiny Monument Records in America (his records were licensed to Decca's London label over here) an his second release *Only The Lonely* hit the top of the charts and paved the way for a run of best sellers which would virtually span the entir decade. Roy was blessed with an incredibly powerful voice encompassing a remarkable range which belied his quietly-spoken, shy person off stage. In 1965, a multi million dollar recording and movie deal saw the 'Big O' leave Monument Records for the mighty MGM althoug Orbison himself insisted that Decca should retain release rights for his U.K. releases. Simultaneously with the American label switch Orbison's traditional major hits became relatively minor ones as his career suffered from the lack of the personal touch which was afforde to his recordings at Monument. He toured the U.K., home to his strongest fan base, well beyond the sixties and was on the threshold of huge comeback in late 1988 when he suffered a fatal heart attack.

**BIGGEST 1964 HIT : *Oh Pretty Woman*.**

**OTHER 60's CHART HITS INCLUDED :**
***Only The Lonely, Running Scared, Dream Baby, In Dreams, Falling, Blue Bayou, It's Over, Pretty Paper, Too Soon To Know.***

**THE SEARCHERS** who were one of the decade's most prolific chart acts.

*ABOVE* - Adam Faith's backing group **THE ROULETTES**
who just missed out on hitting the big time in their own right.

CLIFF BENNETT & THE REBEL ROUSERS
at Hartlepool's Queens Rink Ballroom at the
time of their *One Way Love* chart hit.

Following John Leyton and The Tornados, The Honeycombs became the third act to top the charts with a Joe Meek production when *Have I The Right* climbed to number one.

Incredibly, the chart topping *Go Now* gave The Moody Blues their only top ten outing of the decade.

Chart newcomers The Nashville Teens scored two hits within three months; *Tobacco Road* and *Google Eye*.

Amazingly, Terry Stafford's U.S. smash hit *Suspicion* did not even gain top thirty honours in this country.

Motown artiste Mary Wells hit the charts with her solitary hit *My Guy*. The recording was released in the U.K. on the Stateside label prior to the arrival of Tamla Motown in this country.

# THE HOLLIES

Twenty charts hits during the sixties have justifiably secured The Hollies a permanent place in the annals of pop history. The Manchester based group was formed in 1962 and brought together the talents of Allan Clarke, Graham Nash, Tony Hicks, Eric Haydock and Don Rathbone although Rathbone was replaced on drums by Bobby Elliott in 1963. Soon after their formation, The Hollies signed to EMI's Parlophone label and began building up a solid reputation as a popular live band. Almost instantly, the act began turning out hit singles with a consistency that was the envy of other groups. Their music was as unpretentious as it was infectious with the soaring vocals of Allan Clarke, Tony Hicks and Graham Nash creating one of the most distinctly unique sounds of the British beat group era. By 1966, The Hollies had taken up permanent residency on the British charts with an avalanche of quality singles including the group penned *We're Through*, Goffin & King's *Yes I Will*, the banjo styled *Stop Stop Stop* and the number one hit *I'm Alive*. Unlike many of their rivals, The Hollies did not confine their record successes to the singles charts and their LPs *Stay With The Hollies, Would You Believe, Evolution* and *Hollies Sing Dylan* became best sellers. A Hollies' trademark was always the quality of the 'B' sides of their singles with many of them being at least as good as some 'A' sides on the charts. Even the departures of group members Eric Haydock (in 1966) and Graham Nash (in 1968) failed to halt the group's run of chart successes. The outgoing members were replaced by Bernie Calvert and Terry Sylvester. The hits kept on coming and in some ways reached new artistic peaks as The Hollies added ballads to their repertoire, most notably *He Ain't Heavy He's My Brother*. There then followed a period of unrest and turmoil within the group and Allan Clarke (twice), Sylvester and Calvert left The Hollies. Clarke subsequently re-joined and the nucleus of Clarke, Hicks and Elliott plus supporting musicians plied their hits around the supper club circuit before re-entering the concert hall arena aided and abetted by the re-release of *He Ain't Heavy He's My Brother* which hit top spot on the chart in 1988.

*BIGGEST 1964 HIT : Just One Look.*

*OTHER 60's CHART HITS INCLUDED : Here I Go Again, I'm Alive, Look Through Any Window, I Can't Let Go,
Bus Stop, Stop Stop Stop, On A Carousel, Carrie-Anne, Sorry Suzanne, He Ain't Heavy He's My Brother.*

## Wearside Top Ten ~ 14th January 1964

1. *Glad All Over* ..................... The Dave Clark Five (Columbia)
2. *I Want To Hold Your Hand* ............ The Beatles (Parlophone)
3. *Hippy Hippy Shake* .......... The Swinging Blue Jeans (HMV)
4. *Twenty Four Hours From Tulsa* ...................... Gene Pitney (United Artists)
5. *I Only Want To Be With You* ....... Dusty Springfield (Philips)
6. *Stay* ..................................... The Hollies (Parlophone)
7. *Swinging On A Star* .......................... Big Dee Irwin (Colpix)
8. *I'm The One* ............... Gerry & The Pacemakers (Columbia)
9. *Needles And Pins* ............................... The Searchers (Pye)
10. *Don't Blame Me* ............................... Frank Ifield (Columbia)

## Wearside Top Ten ~ 19th March 1964

1. *Little Children* ...................... Billy J. Kramer & The Dakotas (Parlophone)
2. *Bits And Pieces* ................. The Dave Clark Five (Columbia)
3. *Just One Look* ................................. The Hollies (Parlophone)
4. *Not Fade Away* .......................... The Rolling Stones (Decca)
5. *Anyone Who Had A Heart* .............. Cilla Black (Parlophone)
6. *I Think Of You* .......................... The Merseybeats (Fontana)
7. *Boys Cry* ....................................... Eden Kane (Fontana)
8. *Needles And Pins* ................................. The Searchers (Pye)
9. *That Girl Belongs To Yesterday* ...................... Gene Pitney (United Artists)
10. *Candy Man* ............... Brian Poole & The Tremeloes (Decca)

# THE BEACH BOYS

The Americans only serious contenders to combat the 1963-1965 Merseybeat domination of their charts were The Beach Boys. The group's image was synonymous with sun, surf and beautiful girls and, as such, it was poles apart from the no frills working class persona of the British beat groups. After two years of chart successes in Uncle Sam's domain, The Beach Boys finally struck gold in the U.K. during 1964 with *I Get Around*. The group's line up comprised three brothers (of which Brian Wilson was the group's recognised mentor), a cousin and a school friend. The success of their recordings almost inevitably revolved around Brian Wilson's awesome talent as a writer and producer and indeed he made that his forte from 1965 onwards following his decision to retire from live performances with the group. After four moderately successful British singles in 1965, the group took the first step to matching their American successes with, ironically, one of their lesser efforts, the novelty number *Barbara Ann*. Thereafter followed a string of Brian Wilson masterpieces culminating with the release and immediate number one status of *Good Vibrations,* a recording which took six months, four studios and seventeen recording sessions to perfect. It was around this time that The Beach Boys released their critically acclaimed *Pet Sounds* LP, the sales of which confirmed their superstar status. Exhaustion and alleged drug abuse immediately followed the group's finest hour and their career was thrown into disarray with abortive LP releases and disappointing singles sales. Mid 1968 witnessed a resurgence in popularity as The Beach Boys returned to their roots with the chart topping *Do It Again* and the new found impetus was carried forward to the final year of the decade with two further top ten hits before leaving their record label of seven years, Capitol Records, for pastures new.

**BIGGEST 1964 HIT : I Get Around.**

**OTHER 60's CHART HITS INCLUDED :**
*Sloop John B, God Only Knows, Good Vibrations, Heroes and Villains,*
*Then I Kissed Her, Do It Again, I Can Hear Music, Break Away.*

*ABOVE*
*I Think Of You* was **THE MERSEYBEATS** biggest chart hit.
It made it to number five in 1964.

*RIGHT*
**Top 1964 shows at City Hall, Newcastle.**
**1964 'pop pickers' were spoilt for choice!**

# THE KINKS

One of the most enduring groups to come out of the sixties, The Kinks line-up consisted of brothers Ray and Dave Davies, Peter Quaife and Mick Avory. They were formed in 1963 and their first, and unsuccessful, single was a cover of *Long Tall Sally* but it was not until the release of the Ray Davies song *You Really Got Me* in the summer of 1964 that The Kinks became a household name. The rapidly emerging talents of Ray Davies as one of the country's most thoughtful songwriters ensured a seemingly endless supply of hit material which enabled The Kinks to remain one of the most consistent chart outfits throughout the sixties and into the seventies. Ray Davies' work portrayed him as a brilliantly original songwriter who could move from the almost heavy-metal of *All Day And All Of The Night* to the heavily satirized *Dedicated Follower Of Fashion* with apparent ease. The fun-poking elitism of *Sunny Afternoon* and the thought provoking comment of the plight of the poor on its follow-up *Dead End Street* gave a new dimension to the lyrical side of popular music. As is often the case, genius and eccentricity go hand in hand and throughout the sixties many observers felt that Ray Davies' hand hovered over the self-destruct button too many times for comfort. His tempestuous behaviour and that of the group led to a U.S. ban in 1965 following near violent on-stage antics during a show. Through it all, Davies remained a songwriter of supreme ability and one whose social comment in his songs was accessible to the less scholarly members of society. Bob Dylan eat your heart out! The humour contained within Kinks' records was typically English and was no better exemplified than by the LP, *The Kinks Are The Village Green Preservation Society* while the group's pathos really came to the fore on the 1967 chart hit *Waterloo Sunset*. The Kinks were noticeable by their absence from the charts during 1968 and 1969 although *Lola* and then *Apeman* restored them to chart glory in 1970. Since then, the hits have been sporadic but the group remain a crowd-pulling attraction on the concert hall circuit.

> **BIGGEST 1964 HIT : *You Really Got Me*.**
>
> **OTHER 60's CHART HITS INCLUDED :**
> *All Day And All Of The Night, Tired Of Waiting For You, Set Me Free, Dedicated Follower Of Fashion,*
> *Sunny Afternoon, Waterloo Sunset, Autumn Almanac.*

## *Wearside Top Ten ~ 26th May 1964*

1. *You're My World* ............................ Cilla Black (Parlophone)
2. *Juliet* .............................................. The Four Pennies (Philips)
3. *It's Over* ................................................. Roy Orbison (London)
4. *My Bob Lollipop* ........................................... Millie (Fontana)
5. *Constantly* ........................................ Cliff Richard (Columbia)
6. *A Little Loving* ............................ The Fourmost (Parlophone)
7. *No Particular Place To Go* ......................................................
   Chuck Berry (Pye International)
8. *Don't Throw Your Love Away* ................. The Searchers (Pye)
9. *I Believe* ............................................... The Bachelors (Decca)
10. *The Rise And Fall Of Flingel Bunt* .......................................
    The Shadows (Columbia)

## *Wearside Top Ten ~ 23rd July 1964*

1. *A Hard Day's Night* ........................ The Beatles (Parlophone)
2. *It's All Over Now* ........................ The Rolling Stones (Decca)
3. *I Won't Forget You* .................................... Jim Reeves (RCA)
4. *House Of The Rising Sun* ................ The Animals (Columbia)
5. *I Just Don't Know What To Do With Myself* ..........................
   Dusty Springfield (Philips)
6. *Do Wah Diddy Diddy* ........................ Manfred Mann (HMV)
7. *Hold Me* ..................................................... P.J. Proby (Decca)
8. *Call Up The Groups* ............ The Barron Knights (Columbia)
9. *Tobacco Road* .......................... The Nashville Teens (Decca)
10. *You're No Good* ................ The Swinging Blue Jeans (HMV)

Nightlife in Sunderland really took off in 1964 with Wearsiders spoilt for choice where to spend their hard earned cash. Principal cabaret clubs Wetherells and La Strada were doing a roaring trade with star names of the period. Names appearing at Wetherells included Craig Douglas, Gerry Dorsey (later to find fame as Engelbert Humperdinck), Karl Denver Trio, Ronnie Carroll, Bob Monkhouse and The Vernons Girls while the newly opened La Strada were offering late night revellers the likes of The Kestrels, Vince Hill, Val Doonican, The Seekers and Mike Yarwood. Meanwhile, The Blue Note rounded off the year in fine style with shows starring Gene Vincent, Little Eva and Jerry Lee Lewis. The Odeon continued the year with its big name touring packages including the 'All Stars 64' visit on 20th February featuring John Leyton, Jet Harris, Billie Davis, Mike Sarne, The Rolling Stones, Mike Berry and The Swinging Blue Jeans and on 10th March a star studded bill of Joe Brown, The Crystals, Heinz, Johnny Kidd & The Pirates and Manfred Mann.

Over at The Empire there were visits of Billy J. Kramer & The Dakotas/Gene Pitney/The Fourmost on 28th March and Gerry & The Pacemakers/Helen Shapiro/Danny Williams on 20th September. On a more sour note, the show booked for 29th November starring The Honeycombs and P.J. Proby did not take place as both acts failed to turn up and, as a result, the 100 people booked into the show received a refund.

Other entertainment high spots included the appearance of Adam Faith's backing group The Roulettes at Seaburn Hall as well as the opening of the Bowling Alley in June and the first night party at the Locarno Ballroom on 7th July.

# P.J. PROBY

One of the decade's first extrovert characters, James Marcus Smith, alias P.J. Proby, was born in Houston, Texas on 6th November 1938. Proby first came to Britain in 1964 to appear on the Jack Good produced Around The Beatles television special. The obligatory record release to tie-in with the visit was a raucous revival of the former lilting ballad *Hold Me* which brought Proby to the attention of a multitude of female fans and at the same time provided him with a top three hit record. The follow-up release *Together* was recorded in similar style and also cracked the top ten before it transpired that the artist was still contracted to a previous record company. The change of record label - from Decca to Liberty - coincided with a change in musical direction as he henceforth became the exponent of the epic ballad. Two numbers from West Side Story were made into chart hits by Proby and his career would have undoubtedly benefited from such choice of material had it not been for his on stage antics and the infamous split trousers incident which led to a concert hall and television ban throughout the country. Proby was accused of deliberately splitting his trousers to excite the female audience which in less tolerant times, was labelled obscene. On the back of the adverse publicity he released the appropriately entitled *I Apologise* complete with over-the-top dramatic vocals but the showbiz establishment were not amused. With ongoing bans preventing him from performing regularly, P.J. Proby's career as a recording artist was irreparably damaged. He adopted a somewhat eccentric view of life and became unreliable. He had a run of minor hits during 1966-1968 before declaring himself bankrupt and returning to America. He was very much a wasted talent and it is food for thought to reflect on what might have been.

> **BIGGEST 1964 HIT : Hold Me.**
>
> **OTHER 60's CHART HITS INCLUDED :**
> **Together, Somewhere, I Apologise, Maria, Let The Water Run Down.**

## Wearside Top Ten ~ 1st October 1964

1. I'm Into Something Good ....... Herman's Hermits (Columbia)
2. Rag Doll .................... The Four Seasons (Philips)
3. Oh Pretty Woman ................ Roy Orbison (London)
4. Have I The Right ................ The Honeycombs (Pye)
5. You Really Got Me .................... The Kinks (Pye)
6. Where Did Our Love Go .............. The Supremes (Stateside)
7. As Tears Go By .................. Marianne Faithfull (Decca)
8. The Crying Game ................ Dave Berry (Decca)
9. I Wouldn't Trade You For The World .................... The Bachelors (Decca)
10. The Wedding .................. Julie Rogers (Mercury)

## Wearside Top Ten ~ 10th December 1964

1. I Feel Fine ................... The Beatles (Parlophone)
2. Little Red Rooster ................. The Rolling Stones (Decca)
3. I'm Gonna Be Strong ............... Gene Pitney (Stateside)
4. Downtown ................... Petula Clark (Pye)
5. Baby Love ................... The Supremes (Stateside)
6. Um Um Um Um Um Um ...................... Wayne Fontana & The Mindbenders (Fontana)
7. All Day And All Of The Night ................. The Kinks (Pye)
8. Walk Tall ................... Val Doonican (Decca)
9. Pretty Paper ................. Roy Orbison (London)
10. He's In Town ................ The Rockin' Berries (Pye)

# THE SEARCHERS

Of all the groups to emerge from the initial wave of Merseybeat hysteria, The Searchers' name has demonstrated the greatest longevity as a working group. With minimal personnel changes over the years, the group's touring schedule has not suffered even the slightest hiatus since they first hit the road in 1962. It was during that year that they sent a demo tape of their work to Pye A & R manager Tony Hatch. The group were working in Hamburg at the time alongside dozens of other beat group hopefuls. The following year a Pye recording contract was forthcoming and they quickly began working on a Pomus-Shuman song which had recently been a U.S. hit for The Drifters. The song was *Sweets For My Sweet* and The Searchers' recording of the number featured the close harmonies which were to become the group's hallmark throughout their distinguished chart career. The record was released in August 1963 and stormed to number one within two weeks of release. There then followed a string of hit singles including a further two number ones (one of which was *Needles And Pins*, co-penned by soon-to-be recording star Sonny Bono of Sonny & Cher fame), chart LPs and, unusually, their own fifteen minute weekly show on Radio Luxembourg. By mid 1965 it was apparent that the group's chart topping days were coming to an end although a final top tenner on the Wearside chart, *He's Got No Love*, demonstrated The Searchers' talents as songwriters. The group continued to release quality singles, notably a folk-rock rendition of P.F. Sloan's *Take Me For What I'm Worth* but The Searchers' recording career was destined to follow a parallel path to that of fellow Merseysiders Gerry & The Pacemakers and Billy J. Kramer & The Dakotas for whom mid 1965 was to be a watershed in their collective chart fortunes. More than most beat groups of their genre, The Searchers left the legacy of some of the best expertly crafted harmony pop songs of the mid sixties.

> **BIGGEST 1964 HIT : Needles And Pins.**
>
> **OTHER 60's CHART HITS INCLUDED :**
> **Sweets For My Sweet, Sugar And Spice, Don't Throw Your Love Away, When You Walk In The Room, Goodbye My Love,**
> **What Have They Done To The Rain, Someday We're Gonna Love Again.**

# The Ones That Got Away In ...

**1964**

| | | | | |
|---|---|---|---|---|
| Bad Time | The Roulettes | | I Wonder | The Crystals |
| Suspicion | Terry Stafford | | Like Dreamers Do | The Applejacks |
| It Hurts To Be In Love | Gene Pitney | | What'cha Gonna Do About It | Doris Troy |
| So Much In Love | The Mighty Avengers | | Do What You Do Do Well | Ned Miller |
| She's My Girl | Bobby Shafto | | We'll Sing In The Sunshine | Gale Garnett |
| Only One Such As You | Adam Faith | | | |

Adam Faith's latter day backing group The Roulettes recorded what in retrospect is regarded as one of the British beat era's finest cuts. *Bad Time* was a masterpiece from the pen of Chris Andrews and is a much sought after track today. The fact that it didn't even manage a sniff at the charts remains a mystery.

Meanwhile, The Mighty Avengers recording of the Jagger/Richard song *So Much In Love* unleashed an infectious slice of commercial pop on to vinyl which subsequently confounded everyone when it vanished without trace after a couple of weeks at the bottom end of the top fifty.

Phil Spector temporarily lost the midas touch when The Crystals failed to make it a hat trick of top tenners with *I Wonder* and the little known Doris Troy was unable to convert the turntable hit status of *What'cha Gonna Do About It* into significant sales.

# In 1965 ...

American top three hit *The Birds And The Bees* by Jewel Akens was tipped to repeat its success in Britain but surprisingly stalled at number twenty nine.

Protest singer Joan Baez enjoyed a solitary top ten hit with *There But For Fortune*.

*You've Lost That Lovin' Feelin'* hit the charts twice during the first few weeks of the year. The original version by The Righteous Brothers with epic production by Phil Spector topped the charts while a cover version by Cilla Black made it to number two.

THE BYRDS who hit top spot with *Mr Tambourine Man* in July 1965.

## Wearside Top Ten ~ 11th February 1965

1. *You've Lost That Lovin' Feelin'* .......................................... The Righteous Brothers (London)
2. *Go Now* ......................................... The Moody Blues (Decca)
3. *Tired Of Waiting For You* ......................... The Kinks (Pye)
4. *Keep Searchin'* ........................... Del Shannon (Stateside)
5. *Come Tomorrow* ........................... Manfred Mann (HMV)
6. *I'll Never Find Another You* ................ The Searchers (Pye)
7. *Yeh Yeh* ...................................... Georgie Fame (Columbia)
8. *Leader Of The Pack* ................. The Shangri-Las (Red Bird)
9. *You've Lost That Lovin' Feelin'* ...... Cilla Black (Parlophone)
10. *The Special Years* ............................. Val Doonican (Decca)

## Wearside Top Ten ~ 1st April 1965

1. *The Last Time* ........................... The Rolling Stones (Decca)
2. *Concrete And Clay* ................... Unit Four Plus Two (Decca)
3. *It's Not Unusual* ...................................... Tom Jones (Decca)
4. *Goodbye My Love* ................................. The Searchers (Pye)
5. *For Your Love* ............................. The Yardbirds (Columbia)
6. *The Minute You're Gone* .............. Cliff Richard (Columbia)
7. *I'll Stop At Nothing* ................................. Sandie Shaw (Pye)
8. *I Must Be Seeing Things* ................. Gene Pitney (Stateside)
9. *Silhouettes* ........................... Herman's Hermits (Columbia)
10. *Yes I Will* ...................................... The Hollies (Parlophone)

## BOB DYLAN

Robert Allen Zimmerman engineered cult status for himself during the mid sixties with a collection of songs with ostensibly meaningful lyrics. His disciples preached his gospels, many convinced that his most simple songs contained deeper messages. The self appointed messiah of folk first reached the masses with the 1963 release of the LP *The Freewheelin' Bob Dylan*. This was followed by the protest orientated *The Times They Are A-Changin'* and *Another Side Of Bob Dylan* LPs, both in 1964. All three releases benefited tremendously from The Beatles' well publicised admiration of Dylan's work. The man himself descended upon us for a British tour in January 1965 when his first single, *The Times They Are A-Changin'*, was released to coincide with the visit. Although he was first and foremost an LP artist Dylan released several singles during the mid to late sixties presumably in an attempt to reach a wider audience. Despite being in the genre of his ultimately, almost self indulgent album material, many of his singles had sufficient crossover appeal to make the charts in a big way. Some, such as the less than wonderfully poetic *Maggie's Farm*, did not. The status of the cult hero from Minnesota began to diminish in 1966 after a motorcycle accident forced a prolonged period of inactivity upon Dylan. The record releases became less frequent than of late although other acts continued to successfully cover his songs. As the decade drew to a close, Dylan re-emerged into the spotlight drawing upon country influences for his final two sixties LPs.

**BIGGEST 1965 HIT : *Like A Rolling Stone*.**

**OTHER 60's CHART HITS INCLUDED :**
***The Times They Are A-Changin', Subterranean Homesick Blues, Positively Fourth Street,
Rainy Day Women Nos 12 & 35, Lay Lady Lay.***

# TOM JONES

In 1963, Pontypridd-born Tom Jones formed the group Tommy Scott & The Senators and later recorded some tracks with ace record producer Joe Meek. The following year Jones was taken under the management wing of Gordon Mills (who had been a member of sixties hit makers The Viscounts) who secured a Decca recording contract for his aspiring star. Jones' second record, *It's Not Unusual,* justified Mills' faith in his artist as it rocketed to the top of the Hit Parade and transformed Tom Jones into an immediate sex symbol in the process. The following six singles, although medium sized U.K. hits (including his biggest U.S. hit of the decade *What's New Pussycat*) were something of an anticlimax after the runaway success of *It's Not Unusual* and the impetus of Tom Jones' career appeared to have been dissipated. Drastic action was needed to prevent Tom's dwindling record sales from going into terminal decline and a rapid change of image aimed the Jones' charisma squarely at the more mature end of the pop market. To coincide with the career re-launch in late 1966 Decca released *Green Green Grass Of Home* and the results exceeded everyone's wildest expectations. Nationally the record sold well over one million copies and topped the charts for seven weeks. The skillful image manipulation had worked a treat and Tom Jones was reaching a wider audience than ever before. He stayed with the country flavour for his next single and with ballads in general for the duration of 1967 when his name was rarely out of the best selling lists. Once established as an undisputed megastar he began mixing it with the best of them hopping from ballads to up-tempo numbers and back again. The late sixties was a productive time for Tom Jones as hit singles and LPs came thick and fast both here and in America. He toured regularly in both countries but by 1969 the lure of the dollar proved to be irresistible and for many years Britain was robbed of one of its most outstanding vocal talents as Jones virtually took up residence in Las Vegas.

**BIGGEST 1965 HIT : *It's Not Unusual.***

**OTHER 60's CHART HITS INCLUDED :**
*Green Green Grass Of Home, Detroit City, I'll Never Fall In Love Again, I'm Coming Home, Delilah,*
*Help Yourself, Love Me Tonight, Daughter of Darkness*

Another song to hit the best sellers for two different artists was *Trains And Boats And Planes.* The version featuring the Burt Bacharach Chorus & Orchestra easily outsold the cover version by Billy J. Kramer & The Dakotas.

The Byrds enjoyed their best chart year with three hits including the top tenners *Mr. Tambourine Man* and *All I Really Want To Do.*

Len Barry hit the top three with the song *1-2-3* and released a virtual identikit song for the follow up with *Like A Baby.*

# GENE PITNEY

Gene Pitney's first taste of British chart success was in 1961 as a songwriter when he penned hits for Ricky Nelson (*Hello Mary Lou*) and Bobby Vee (*Rubber Ball*). The timing of his emergence in Britain as a performer of big ballads coincided, almost uniquely, with the arrival of Merseybeat. Not only did the clean-cut American nestle comfortably in the charts alongside the long haired beat groups of the day but after meeting The Rolling Stones he recorded the Jagger-Richards song *That Girl Belongs To Yesterday* and took it to number seven on the hit parade. Pitney had been a successful recording artist in his native America for some time when he visited the U.K. for a promotional tour in January 1964 to tie-in with the release of *Twenty Four Hours From Tulsa.* Following the top five chart placing of that record, Gene Pitney became a regular visitor to our shores and our charts. He toured the country regularly, often appearing on the same bills as the likes of The Rolling Stones and Status Quo and between 1964 and 1967 he notched up an impressive ten top ten singles. His extraordinary vocal range endeared him to the top songwriters of the day and during his hit making period was able to hand-pick his songs for single releases from the rich catalogues of Bacharach-David, Mann-Weil and Randy Newman. At a time when albums were not considered to be the art form which they are today, some artists consigned 'B' sides of their singles and what they considered to be sub-standard material to their LP releases. Conversely, Gene Pitney lavished as much care and attention to his 'B' sides and LP tracks as to his 'A' sides with the consequence that he hit the LP charts on several occasions. By the late sixties, rock music had begun to take a stranglehold on the charts and the expertly crafted three minute ballad, Pitney's forte, became passé almost overnight. He continued to enjoy minor hits well into the seventies and his six-monthly U.K. tours became the norm. He unexpectedly topped the charts as guest vocalist to Marc Almond on a 1988 re-cut of *Something's Gotten Hold Of My Heart.*

**BIGGEST 1965 HIT : *Looking Through The Eyes Of Love.***

**OTHER 60's CHART HITS INCLUDED :**
*Twenty Four Hours From Tulsa, I'm Gonna Be Strong, I Must Be Seeing Things, Backstage,*
*Nobody Needs Your Love, Something's Gotten Hold Of My Heart.*

THE DIXIE CUPS who deserved more than their moderate
U.K. chart placings with *Chapel Of Love* and *Iko Iko*.

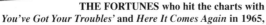
THE FORTUNES who hit the charts with
*You've Got Your Troubles'* and *Here It Comes Again* in 1965,

# SONNY & CHER

Throughout the early sixties the American recording industry successfully exported an abundance of teen idols, well groomed with coy smiles and boy-next-door images. The sudden emergence of British beat groups turned the music business on its head as it sowed the seeds of a youth revolution which was instantly dismissive of what it perceived as the 'establishment' face of popular music. For a while the American recording industry was left reeling. Eventually, in an attempt to re-gain lost ground, the Americans unleashed their own teen rebels on to vinyl. One of their first - and finest - examples was Sonny & Cher, two hairies with a hippy style of dress and a bohemian lifestyle to match. The pair were married in 1964 and after several early recording sessions proved to be unfruitful, the duo recorded *I Got You Babe* (written and produced by Sonny) which brought them instant Transatlantic fame as it topped the charts on both sides of the ocean. Sonny & Cher were a publicist's dream as their unconventional behaviour cocked a snook at the establishment and its out of date values. The duo's high profile and uniquely commercial style of folk rock ensured ongoing vinyl successes including chart entries as soloists for Sonny with *Laugh At Me* (1965) and Cher with the Byrds' inspired *All I Really Want To Do* (1965) and *Bang Bang* (1966). By 1967 the hits had all but dried up as Sonny & Cher's music failed to move with the times and their antics, once regarded outrageous, now considered to be almost sublime by a youth movement heading towards the 'Summer Of Love' and all its permissive implications. They saw out the decade with two low budget movies before moving on to the cabaret circuit. They were divorced in 1974 with Cher later emerging as a major force as an actress and singer.

> **BIGGEST 1965 HIT : I Got You Babe.**
>
> **OTHER 60's CHART HITS INCLUDED :**
> **Baby Don't Go, But You're Mine, What Now My Love,**
> **Little Man, The Beat Goes On.**

Surprise number one of the year was Ken Dodd's *Tears*.

Matt Monro's recording of Lennon & McCartney's *Yesterday* gave the balladeer his fifth and final top ten hit of the decade.

Peter & Gordon revived The Teddy Bears' fifties hit *To Know Him Is To Love Him* as *To Know You Is To Love You* to give the duo their fourth top ten hit.

There were two number ones for The Seekers; I*'ll Never Find Another You* and *The Carnival Is Over*.

# THE ROLLING STONES

Initially The Rollin' Stones; by early 1963 the group added a 'g' to their name and consisted of the eventual line up of Mick Jagger, Keith Richard, Brian Jones, Bill Wyman and Charlie Watts. They signed a management deal with flamboyant sixties entrepreneur Andrew Loog Oldham, a recording deal with Decca Records and paraded their debut single *Come On* to an unsuspecting British public on television's Thank Your Lucky Stars in June 1963. The record was only a minor hit. Armed with a nugget of gold - an unrecorded Lennon-McCartney song - for their next single, The Rolling Stones released *I Wanna Be Your Man* in late 1963 immediately after their supporting role on tour with The Everly Brothers and they scraped into the lower reaches of Wearside's Top Ten. By early 1964 the group were headlining on tour with The Ronettes and, following the top three hit *Not Fade Away,* they managed to score five consecutive number ones to make the act one of the hottest properties around and second only to The Beatles. With Oldham's cleverly engineered rebellious image for Mick & Co and Decca's determination to succeed with the group in the wake of missing out on The Beatles, the group's infectious blend of R & B and pop simply could not fail. The irreverent behaviour of the group alienated them to the older generation while enhancing their appeal to their teenage following; sell-out tours, hit singles and albums abounded both here and in the States; The Rolling Stones were in danger of becoming an institution! In 1967 the group made their only appearance on top television show Sunday Night At The London Palladium and committed the ultimate indiscretion of refusing to stand on the revolving stage waving to the audience during the programme's fade out! As the decade drew to a close the group's record releases became sporadic but were, nonetheless, as successful as ever.

> *BIGGEST 1965 HIT : The Last Time.*
>
> *OTHER 60's CHART HITS INCLUDED :*
> *It's All Over Now, Little Red Rooster, (I Can't Get No) Satisfaction,*
> *Get Off Of My Cloud, Paint It Black, Jumping Jack Flash,*
> *Honky Tonk Women, Brown Sugar.*

America fought back as the chart invasion by British beat groups dominated every corner of the globe. The suitably rebellious Sonny & Cher were introduced to the music world and justifiably shot to stardom - and the top of the charts - with *I Got You Babe.*

Chart newcomers Unit Four Plus Two topped the Hit Parade with *Concrete And Clay* and followed it up with *You've Never Been In Love Like This Before* before slipping into chart obscurity.

The Walker Brothers made their chart debut with *Love Her* and subsequently scored with two of the year's biggest hits, *Make It Easy On Yourself* and *My Ship Is Coming In.*

The Yardbirds enjoyed their best chart year with three top five hits; *For Your Love, Heart Full Of Soul* and the double 'A' sided *Evil Hearted You/Still I'm Sad.*

## Wearside Top Ten ~ 27th May 1965

1. Long Live Love ............................ Sandie Shaw (Pye)
2. Where Are You Now (My Love) ............... Jackie Trent (Pye)
3. King Of The Road ......................... Roger Miller (Philips)
4. True Love Ways ........................... Peter & Gordon (Columbia)
5. World Of Our Own ......................... The Seekers (Columbia)
6. Poor Man's Son ........................... The Rockin' Berries (Pye)
7. Ticket To Ride ........................... The Beatles (Parlophone)
8. This Little Bird ......................... Marianne Faithfull (Decca)
9. The Clapping Song ........................ Shirley Ellis (London)
10. Wonderful World ......................... Herman's Hermits (Columbia)

## Wearside Top Ten ~ 5th August 1965

1. Mr. Tambourine Man ...................... The Byrds (CBS)
2. Help .................................... The Beatles (Parlophone)
3. You've Got Your Troubles ................ The Fortunes (Decca)
4. Tossing And Turning ..................... The Ivy League (Piccadilly)
5. Catch Us If You Can ..................... The Dave Clark Five (Columbia)
6. We Gotta Get Out Of This Place .......... The Animals (Columbia)
7. I'm Alive ............................... The Hollies (Parlophone)
8. Heart Full Of Soul ...................... The Yardbirds (Columbia)
9. In The Middle Of Nowhere ............... Dusty Springfield (Philips)
10. To Know You Is To Love You ............. Peter & Gordon (Columbia)

## Wearside Top Ten ~ 7th October 1965

1. *Tears* ..................................................... Ken Dodd (Columbia)
2. *Make It Easy On Yourself* ....... The Walker Brothers (Philips)
3. *Eve Of Destruction* ............................ Barry McGuire (RCA)
4. *If You Gotta Go Go Now* .................... Manfred Mann (HMV)
5. *Hang On Sloopy* ........................... The McCoys (Immediate)
6. *Almost There* ...................................... Andy Williams (CBS)
7. *I Got You Babe* .............................. Sonny & Cher (Atlantic)
8. *Look Through Any Window* ........... The Hollies (Parlophone)
9. *(I Can't Get No) Satisfaction* ...... The Rolling Stones (Decca)
10. *Message Understood* ............................... Sandie Shaw (Pye)

## Wearside Top Ten ~ 23rd December 1965

1. *Day Tripper/We Can Work It Out* ...................................... The Beatles (Parlophone)
2. *The River* .................................................... Ken Dodd (Columbia)
3. *Wind Me Up* .................................... Cliff Richard (Columbia)
4. *The Carnival Is Over* .................... The Seekers (Columbia)
5. *My Ship Is Coming In* ........... The Walker Brothers (Philips)
6. *My Generation* ...................................... The Who (Brunswick)
7. *1-2-3* ............................................... Len Barry (Brunswick)
8. *Tears* ................................................... Ken Dodd (Columbia)
9. *Let's Hang On* ........................... The Four Seasons (Philips)
10. *A Lover's Concerto* ........................... The Toys (Stateside)

# THE WALKER BROTHERS

Scott Engel, John Maus and Garry Leeds first met up in Los Angeles in the summer of 1964 and by February 1965 they arrived in Britain as The Walker Brothers and signed to Philips Records. After the failure of their first record, the image of the group was re-structured with Scott assuming the role of front man. His dramatic vocals coupled with his good looks assured him - and the group - of a strong female fan following. The outfit's second release was a revival of an earlier Everly Brothers' track *Love Her* and became a minor chart hit. The Walker Brothers subsequently took to the road as a live act with Engel and Maus sharing the spotlight on vocals while Leeds became the centrepiece of the backing group. With the benefit of the Burt Bacharach/Hal David blockbuster *Make It Easy On Yourself,* The Walker Brothers became overnight recording sensations as they stormed to the coveted number one spot. Concurrently with this success the various teen magazines clamoured for photographs and stories about the act as they sensed a readership of hysterical female fans with an insatiable appetite for Walker Brothers' news. With two further massive hits including another number one and the mega selling LP *Take It Easy With The Walker Brothers,* the group were sitting on top of the world and could seemingly do no wrong. A successful U.K. tour with The Troggs and Dave Dee, Dozy, Beaky, Mick & Tich reinforced the popularity of Engel, Maus and Leeds although the relatively poor showing of their fifth hit did give some cause for concern. After two subsequent releases failed to register in the customary higher echelons of the charts, the inevitable cracks began to appear as personal conflicts combined to tear the act apart. A 'Farewell Tour' (which also starred Cat Stevens, Engelbert Humperdinck and The Jimi Hendrix Experience) in March 1967 followed by the best selling *Images* LP in April and the sadly ignored *Walking In The Rain* single in May signalled the end of The Walker Brothers' sixties adventure.

> **BIGGEST 1965 HIT : *Make It Easy On Yourself*.**
>
> **OTHER 60's CHART HITS INCLUDED :**
> ***My Ship Is Coming In, The Sun Ain't Gonna Shine Anymore,***
> ***(Baby) You Don't Have To Tell Me, Another Tear Falls.***

The Tamla Motown label was first launched in Britain. Prior to the launch, U.S. Motown hits were released i Britain on a variety of record labels including Oriole, London and Stateside.

The nightlife scene in Sunderland kept buzzing throughout 1965 with night clubs Wetherells, La Strada, Blu Note, Club Ro-KoKo, and the newly refurbished Top Rank Suite all presenting a galaxy of chart names t entertain Wearsiders. In addition there were also shows being staged at Seaburn Hall, Bay Hotel, Odeon an Empire Theatre.

Cabaret names at Wetherells included Tom Jones, Lulu & The Luvvers, Georgie Fame, The Barron Knight Dave Allen, Johnnie Ray, Danny Williams, Susan Maughan and Mike Sarne. Over at the La Strada there w Lonnie Donegan, Helen Shapiro, Joe Brown & His Bruvvers, The Caravelles, The Migil Five and Des O'Conno

*He's In Town* (1964) and *Poor Man's Son* (1965) represented
THE ROCKIN' BERRIES two moments of chart glory.

The recently opened Blue Note were advertising their show on 15th January with The Fortunes as "London's Top Cabaret Group".

Also at the Blue Note in June, for more contemporary tastes, there was The Spencer Davis Group.

The Odeon had what was arguably the show of the year in Sunderland with a star studded bill featuring The Rolling Stones, The Hollies, Dave Berry & The Cruisers and Goldie & The Gingerbreads. It was also at the Odeon that The Beatles' film 'Help' opened on 2nd August.

Other goodies to keep the 1965 'pop pickers' happy included The Fourmost and P.J. Proby at the Empire, Unit Four Plus Two at Seaburn Hall, The Brook Brothers and The Lorne Gibson Trio at Club Ro-KoKo plus Johnny Duncan at the Bay Hotel.

## *The Ones That Got Away In ...*

| | |
|---|---|
| *Upon A Painted Ocean* ........................ Barry McGuire | *(Say) You're My Girl* ........................ Roy Orbison |
| *Voodoo Woman* ................................ Bobby Goldsboro | *The In Crowd* ...................................... Dobie Gray |
| *She's Just My Style* ......... Gary Lewis & The Playboys | *The Birds & The Bees* ....................... Jewel Akens |
| *We Didn't Ask To Be Brought Here* ......... Bobby Darin | *Diane From Manchester Square* ....... Tommy Roe |
| *Sins Of The Family* ...................................... P.F. Sloan | *Keep On Trying* ..................................... Bobby Vee |
| *The World Through A Tear* ....................... Neil Sedaka | |

By 1965, former American chart stalwarts were fighting a losing battle in their attempts to regain lost ground with British record buyers. Bobby Vee, Neil Sedaka, Roy Orbison, Bobby Darin and Tommy Roe all continued to release excellent commercial singles but, with a new generation of record buyers turning their attentions elsewhere, the records were ignored.

The British public's appetite for protest songs appeared to be abating when Barry McGuire's follow-up to *Eve Of Destruction* failed to chart and composer P.F. Sloan's *Sins Of The Family* made only the briefest appearance on the top fifty.

Two commercial soul singles which were strong U.S. sellers and deserved similar sales over here were *The Birds And The Bees* (Jewel Akens) and *The In Crowd* (Dobie Gray).

# In 1966 ...

Eddy Arnold scored a surprise country hit with *Make The World Go Away.*

Spanish/German outfit Los Bravos enjoyed two brief moments of fame with the hits *Black Is Black* and *I Don't Care.*

Lou Christie's falsetto vocals gave him a chart debut with *Lightnin' Strikes.*

Two versions of *Sunny* made the charts; the original American hit by Bobby Hebb and Georgie Fame's British cover version.

Ex Manfred Mann lead singer Paul Jones made his chart debut as a soloist with *High Time.*

The Lovin' Spoonful first hit the charts with *Daydream* and quickly followed it up with *Summer In The City.*

*California Dreamin'*, *Monday Monday* and *I Saw Her Again* established The Mamas & The Papas as chart artists in both Britain and America. The hits continued when both *Dedicated To The One I Love* and *Creeque Alley* became major hits during the 'Summer Of Love'.

Happy memories of the halcyon days at the
Top Rank Suite and Locarno ballrooms in Sunderland.
These two shows took place in 1966

*LEFT*
Club Latino opened in South Shields in January 1966 to become the region's first premier cabaret spot.
It represented an investment of £200,000 for the Bailey Organisation who operated a chain of north east night clubs during the sixties.

*RIGHT*
In *Please Stay* THE CRYIN' SHAMES produced one of the best record releases of 1966; the year which saw them playing at La Cubana in Sunderland.

After leaving The Animals, Alan Price made the top ten at the first attempt as The Alan Price Set with *I Put A Spell On You.*

Billy Fury's tremendous run of twenty three consecutive hit singles came to an end when *Don't Let A Little Pride Stand In Your Way* failed to make any impression on the charts.

Paul Simon saw two of his songs in the top ten chart in May; *The Sound of Silence* (The Bachelors) and *Homeward Bound* (Simon & Garfunkel).

It was a good year for the Sinatras. Nancy topped the charts in March with *These Boots Are Made For Walkin'* and Frank repeated the achievement in June with *Strangers In The Night.*

# SIMON & GARFUNKEL

The celebrated duo who rose to international prominence in the mid sixties by combining the thinking man's lyrics with melodic music and close harmonies. Paul Simon and Art Garfunkel first fused their undoubted talent as Tom & Jerry in 1957 and achieved minor U.S. success under that pseudonym before pursuing various less successful solo projects. The duo reunited briefly in 1964 during the early days of the folk/rock boom and recorded an LP, *Wednesday Morning 3 am.*, of mainly acoustic material. One of the LP's tracks was *The Sound Of Silence* and, without informing Simon & Garfunkel, CBS A & R manager Tom Wilson re-mixed the track by adding electric guitar, drums and percussion and released the result as a single in 1965. The record topped the U.S. charts (in the U.K. it was successfully covered by The Bachelors, much to Paul Simon's annoyance) and the duo were rushed into the recording studio to prepare an LP, *Sounds Of Silence*, which included some of the act's finest works; *Homeward Bound* (which became their first U.K. hit single), *I Am A Rock* and *A Most Peculiar Man*. Both artists were influenced by The Everly Brothers during their formative years and their close harmony vocals of later years bore testament to that fact. There then followed several classic albums which justifiably secured Simon & Garfunkel a huge Transatlantic following, predominantly with the student population. *Parsley, Sage, Rosemary And Thyme* (1966), *The Graduate* (1968) and *Bookends* (1969) contained some absolute jewels which rivalled the works of any other composers of the period. Sell out concerts at London's Royal Albert Hall in July 1968 reaffirmed their vast popularity. Lyrically the two acts were poles apart, The Everlys singing largely about teenage romance while Simon & Garfunkel's work was inevitably cloaked with social comment of one type or another. Although the albums sold well, hit singles did not come readily in this country. However, the end of the decade saw both the single and EP versions of *Mrs. Robinson* chart in a major way, as did *The Boxer* and *Bridge Over Troubled Water,* although the latter's phenomenal sales did not begin to register until the early weeks of 1970.

> **BIGGEST 1966 HIT : Homeward Bound.**
>
> **OTHER 60's CHART HITS INCLUDED :**
> *I Am A Rock, Mrs. Robinson, The Boxer.*

## Wearside Top Ten ~ 15th February 1966

1. *Nineteenth Nervous Breakdown* ........................................... The Rolling Stones (Decca)
2. *These Boots Are Made For Walking* ...................................... Nancy Sinatra (Reprise)
3. *You Were On My Mind* ................. Crispian St. Peters (Decca)
4. *A Groovy Kind Of Love* ............. The Mindbenders (Fontana)
5. *Love's Just A Broken Heart* ............ Cilla Black (Parlophone)
6. *My Love* ..................................................... Petula Clark (Pye)
7. *Michelle* ......................................... The Overlanders (Pye)
8. *Mirror Mirror* ............ Pinkerton's Assorted Colours (Decca)
9. *Spanish Flea* ..................... Herb Alpert (Pye International)
10. *Inside-Looking Out* ............................... The Animals (Decca)

## Wearside Top Ten ~ 26th April 1966

1. *You Don't Have To Say You Love Me* ...................................... Dusty Springfield (Philips)
2. *Bang Bang (My Baby Shot Me Down)* ........... Cher (Liberty)
3. *Pretty Flamingo* ................................. Manfred Mann (HMV)
4. *Daydream* .............. The Lovin' Spoonful (Pye International)
5. *Hold Tight* ....................................................................... Dave Dee, Dozy, Beaky, Mick & Tich (Fontana)
6. *Somebody Help Me* .............. Spencer Davis Group (Fontana)
7. *Pied Piper* .................................... Crispian St. Peters (Decca)
8. *Alfie* .................................................. Cilla Black (Parlophone)
9. *The Sound Of Silence* ......................... The Bachelors (Decca)
10. *Substitute* .................................................. The Who (Reaction)

*ABOVE* - **Major touring packages to visit City Hall, Newcastle in 1965 including the mis-spelt EVERLY BROTHERS**

*LEFT* - **THE YARDBIRDS who enjoyed major chart successes during the mid sixties.**

# SMALL FACES

Small Faces fronted by Steve Marriott burst on to the scene in 1965 as exponents of the Mod/R & B style of music which was initially popularised in the mid sixties by The Who. Inexorably part of the Mod movement, Small Faces were christened as a result of their slight physical stature and the mod connotation of the word 'face'. They were signed to Decca Records in 1965 and cracked the charts with their first single release *What'cha Gonna Do About It*. After a slight chart hiatus, they emerged as a major recording act in 1966 with four solid top ten hits including the chart topping *All Or Nothing* which was written by group members Steve Marriott and Ronnie Lane. The group's first LP *The Small Faces* became one of the year's biggest sellers, peaking at number three and staying on the charts for twenty five weeks. With disagreements abounding between the group, their management and their record company, as well as a ban from Top Of The Pops, Small Faces' career suffered in the short term with only two moderately successful singles by recent standards during the first half of 1967. With the group signed to Immediate Records (owned by manager Andrew Oldham), they briefly entered the psychedelic arena with one of the two previously mentioned 1967 singles, *Here Come The Nice,* as well as the massive seller *Itchycoo Park*. As if intentionally diversifying in their choice of singles, the group then returned to their blues roots for the penultimate top ten hit of the decade before finally rounding off their chart adventures with a Kinks like music hall inspired rocker. Small Faces were not just a singles group and they enjoyed two chart LPs while signed to the Immediate label. These were *Small Faces,* a confusingly similar title to the earlier Decca LP *The Small Faces* (the group themselves never used the word 'The' in their billing) and the critically acclaimed concept LP *Ogden's Nut Gone Flake* which topped the LP charts for several weeks without the benefit of the act's on stage endorsement of it as they refused to play most of the tracks in their live stage act.

> **BIGGEST 1966 HIT : All Or Nothing.**
>
> **OTHER 60's CHART HITS INCLUDED :**
> **Sha La La La Lee, Hey Girl, My Mind's Eye, Itchycoo Park, Tin Soldier, Lazy Sunday.**

## Wearside Top Ten ~ 5th July 1966

1. *Sunny Afternoon* ............................................ The Kinks (Pye)
2. *Nobody Needs Your Love* ................... Gene Pitney (Stateside)
3. *Paperback Writer* ........................... The Beatles (Parlophone)
4. *Bus Stop* ...................................... The Hollies (Parlophone)
5. *River Deep Mountain High* ....... Ike & Tina Turner (London)
6. *Strangers In The Night* ...................... Frank Sinatra (Reprise)
7. *Get Away* ....................................... Georgie Fame (Columbia)
8. *Hideaway* ... Dave Dee, Dozy, Beaky, Mick & Tich (Fontana)
9. *I Couldn't Live Without Your Love* ............ Petula Clark (Pye)
10. *Don't Answer Me* ............................. Cilla Black (Parlophone)

## Wearside Top Ten ~ 6th September 1966

1. *All Or Nothing* ...................................... Small Faces (Decca)
2. *Eleanor Rigby/Yellow Submarine* .. The Beatles (Parlophone)
3. *God Only Knows* .......................... The Beach Boys (Capitol)
4. *Too Soon To Know* ............................. Roy Orbison (London)
5. *They're Coming To Take Me Away Ha-Haaa!* ....................... Napoleon XIV (Warner Bros.)
6. *Distant Drums* ............................................ Jim Reeves (RCA)
7. *Lovers Of The World Unite* .... David & Jonathan (Columbia)
8. *Mama* ...................................................... Dave Berry (Decca)
9. *Got To Get You Into My Life* ............................................... Cliff Bennett & The Rebel Rousers (Parlophone)
10. *A Girl Like You* ...................................... The Troggs (Fontana)

# DAVE DEE, DOZY, BEAKY, MICK & TICH

The group with one of the longest names on the charts, Dave Dee, Dozy, Beaky, Mick & Tich shared the common training ground of many of their beat group rivals - Hamburg clubland. The act distinguished itself from others in that their live rock and roll based show was laced with comedy routines some of which were slightly racy for the period. In 1964 they played as resident group at Butlin's Clacton-on-Sea before graduating to supporting The Honeycombs on tour. The Honeycombs' management team of Ken Howard and Alan Blaikley were so impressed with Dave Dee and Company that they signed them to a management contract and ultimately penned each of the group's catalogue of hit singles. After signing to Fontana Records the group released two flop singles before debuting in the lower reaches of the chart during the final week of 1965 with *You Make It Move*. This most colourful of sixties groups brought a touch of the theatre to pop with, at times, outlandish stage attire and three minute melodramatic sketches to accompany each song. The songs themselves were as varied as any group's repertoire at the time; from the foot stomping beat of *Hold Tight* to the Greek influence of *Bend It*, from the Latin American type arrangement of *The Legend Of Xanadu* to the tongue on cheek Caribbean sounding *Zabadak* with totally nonsensical lyrics. In retrospect, each single was a mini masterpiece which owed not one iota to any prevailing musical trend. The diversity of the material doubtless played a role in enhancing the longevity of this most unpretentious of groups. The supreme irony is that it may well have been that very diversity that sounded the death knell of the group's chart career. Having exhausted the number of musical options open to them at the time and with no sound to truly call their own, the hits finally dried up in 1969 and the fans called time on Dave Dee, Dozy, Beaky, Mick & Tich shortly afterwards.

> **BIGGEST 1966 HIT : Bend It.**
>
> **OTHER 60's CHART HITS INCLUDED :**
> **Hold Tight, Save Me, Hideaway, Okay, Zabadak, The Legend of Xanadu, Last Night In Soho.**

Elvis Presley successfully revived Ketty Lester's 1962 hit *Love Letters*.

*Reach Out I'll Be There* by The Four Tops displaced Jim Reeves' long running chart topper *Distant Drums*.

Tom Jones had his biggest selling British single with *Green Green Grass Of Home*.

It was quite a year for live entertainment in the north east. Top touring packages to visit City Hall in Newcastle included Roy Orbison/The Walker Brothers, The Kinks and The Rolling Stones/Ike & Tina Turner/The Yardbirds. Cabaret was thriving in Sunderland with The Hollies, The Searchers, Sandie Shaw and Gerry & The Pacemakers at Wetherells while Millie, The Rockin' Berries, Lonnie Donegan and Engelbert Humperdinck played at La Strada. La Cubana catered for more current tastes with appearances by The Spencer Davis Group, Alan Price and Long John Baldry.

In Sunderland, The Empire Theatre played host to The Who while ballroom pop concerts included The Swinging Blue Jeans, The Kinks, The Mindbenders and Billy J Kramer & The Dakotas (at Locarno) and Small Faces, The Troggs, The Pretty Things and Johnny Kidd & The Pirates (at Top Rank Suite). Tragically, Johnny Kidd was killed on 6th October 1966, six months after his Sunderland show.

The year saw drinks licences granted for the Porama Club in High Street West, the Safari Club in Albion Place as well as the Black Cat Club and the Roker Park Club at Roker (all Sunderland).

## THE FOUR TOPS

The Four Tops remain one of the finest ever exponents of Motown music. The group originally worked as The Four Aims as they sang their way around the supper club circuit in Detroit during the mid fifties. A subsequent name change and a series of one-off recording deals brought little success until 1963 when they joined the Motown organisation as session singers. Within a year they were signed to the label in their own right and paired with the writing/production team of Holland-Dozier-Holland. The chemistry worked instantly in America but took a little longer in this country. By 1965, the Tamla Motown label had its own identity in the U.K. (having been previously released principally on EMI's Stateside label) and the first of a string of Four Tops' classics dented the charts. From this point onwards the outfit grew in stature with every release and confirmed their popularity in the U.K. with a sold out tour which had been arranged by Brian Epstein. The classic Motown sounding *Reach Out I'll Be There* created a milestone in the group's career when it became their biggest worldwide hit to date and their only U.K. chart topper. It undoubtedly represented the pinnacle of success for The Four Tops/Holland-Dozier-Holland collaboration. The group then took their career off on to a tangent as they temporarily abandoned their traditional Motown sound in their search of an even wider audience. The experimentation of recording soul versions of earlier pop hits worked well and ensured an avoidance of the musical typecasting which had befallen some of their fellow Motown artists. Their versions of *Walk Away Renee* and *If I Were A Carpenter* exuded a new found freshness thanks to the Holland-Dozier-Holland productions which justifiably gave the songs a new lease of life. Ironically it was the departure of that production team from the Motown ranks which temporarily left The Four Tops in the doldrums for the final eighteen months of the decade. Fortunately, the group recovered to re-assert themselves as significant recording stars of the seventies and eighties. There can however be little doubting that most of The Four Tops' classics were firmly entrenched in the sixties.

*BIGGEST 1966 HIT : Reach Out I'll Be There.*

*OTHER 60's CHART HITS INCLUDED : I Can't Help Myself, Standing In The Shadows Of Love, Bernadette,*
*Walk Away Renee, If I Were A Carpenter, Seven Rooms Of Gloom, Do What You Gotta Do.*

# THE SUPREMES

The Supremes are America's most successful female vocal group of all time. From humble beginnings as The Primettes in 1959, the act gradually evolved into The Supremes comprising Diana Ross, Mary Wilson and Florence Ballard. After a series of flop singles, Ballard was replaced by Ross as the group's lead singer and soon afterwards the act broke into the U.S. charts. After the follow-up failed to sell, Motown chief Berry Gordy teamed the girls with up and coming record producers Holland-Dozier-Holland. The move instantly triggered a remarkable run of successes which started with the Transatlantic hit *Where Did Our Love Go* and encompassed such sixties Motown gems as *Baby Love, Come See About Me* and *Stop In The Name Of Love* all of which were simply constructed songs, built around an irresistible disco beat and great hook lines. In March 1965, The Supremes topped the bill on a U.K. package tour (which also starred Stevie Wonder, Martha & The Vandellas, The Temptations and The Miracles) which was set up to launch the Motown label in this country. At this point there was a career move towards a more sophisticated presentation as the girls talents blossomed concurrently with those of Holland-Dozier-Holland and they began recording ambitious LP projects such as their collection of Broadway standards. They also starred at the prestigious Copacabana in New York and assumed the roll of polished, all-round entertainers. By 1967, unrest in the group saw the unceremonious removal of Florence Ballard from the group (for allegedly troublesome behaviour) and the elevation of Diana Ross to star billing on The Supremes' records. Ballard's successor was Cindy Birdsong who was slotted into the line up without public mention. The departure of Motown's premier production team disrupted the girls' run of U.K. hits during 1968 and early 1969 when their releases only made the lower reaches of the charts. Diana Ross left the group in 1969 and their final, poignant appearance together was on American TV's Ed Sullivan Show singing *Someday We'll Be Together* on December 21st of that year. The Supremes re-formed and scored five consecutive U.K. chart hits during the early seventies while Diana Ross progressed to superstar status.

> **BIGGEST 1966 HIT : *You Can't Hurry Love*.**
>
> **OTHER 60's CHART HITS INCLUDED :**
> ***Where Did Our Love Go, Baby Love, Stop In The Name Of Love, You Keep Me Hangin' On, The Happening, Reflections.***

## *Wearside Top Ten ~ 3rd November 1966*

1. *Reach Out I'll Be There* ...... The Four Tops (Tamla Motown)
2. *I Can't Control Myself* ...................... The Troggs (Page One)
3. *Stop Stop Stop* ................................. The Hollies (Parlophone)
4. *Distant Drums* ................................. Jim Reeves (RCA)
5. *High Time* ................................... Paul Jones (HMV)
6. *Winchester Cathedral* .......... New Vaudeville Band (Fontana)
7. *Bend It* ....... Dave Dee, Dozy, Beaky, Mick & Tich (Fontana)
8. *No Milk Today* ...................... Herman's Hermits (Columbia)
9. *I'm A Boy* ................................... The Who (Reaction)
10. *Semi Detached Suburban Mr. Jones* ........................ Manfred Mann (Fontana)

## *Wearside Top Ten ~ 29th December 1966*

1. *Green Green Grass Of Home* .................. Tom Jones (Decca)
2. *Morningtown Ride* .......................... The Seekers (Columbia)
3. *What Would I Be* ................................. Val Doonican (Decca)
4. *Sunshine Superman* ........................................ Donovan (Pye)
5. *Dead End Street* ........................................... The Kinks (Pye)
6. *Friday On My Mind* .............. The Easybeats (United Artists)
7. *Save Me* ..... Dave Dee, Dozy, Beaky, Mick & Tich (Fontana)
8. *Good Vibrations* .......................... The Beach Boys (Capitol)
9. *My Mind's Eye* ....................................... Small Faces (Decca)
10. *You Keep Me Hangin' On* .... The Supremes (Tamla Motown)

# THE TROGGS

Originally known as The Troglodytes with Reg Ball on lead vocals, the group were signed up by The Kinks' manager Larry Page in 1965 whereupon their name was abbreviated to The Troggs and Ball courted publicity by changing his name to Presley. The group made rawness of sound into their trademark and almost elevated it into an art form throughout a distinguished yet short chart career which spawned a creditable five top ten hits in eighteen months. After one flop single, the group recorded the lyrically banal *Wild Thing* which catapulted them to stardom on its route to number two in the charts. The follow-up, *With A Girl Like You,* went one better and topped the U.K. charts before inadvertently becoming the centre of a major row in America after the record company incorrectly coupled it with *Wild Thing* on the same single. After three similarly sounding singles, The Troggs opted for a gentler approach for their next release before tinkering with mild psychedelia on a subsequent recording. Throughout their chart career the group opted for a polite, almost naive country bumkin image which was seen to epitomise their west country roots while being at odds with the blatant sexuality of some of their songs. The Troggs last stab at the charts was towards the end of 1967 with the ballad *Love Is All Around,* a song with lasting appeal as witnessed by its revival at the hands of Wet Wet Wet almost thirty years later. The group's career hit a downward spiral after a fall out with their manager culminated in a High Court case. They continued to work on the cabaret club and college circuits until the end of the decade when the inevitable group split occurred, leaving the members to pursue various solo projects.

> **BIGGEST 1966 HIT : *With A Girl Like You*.**
>
> **OTHER 60's CHART HITS INCLUDED :**
> ***Wild Thing, I Can't Control Myself, Anyway That You Want Me, Give It To Me, Love Is All Around.***

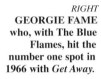

It was around this time that Wearsider John Alpin began promoting pop concerts in Sunderland, principally at the Bay Hotel. Names included Family, Bluesology (featuring Long John Baldry and Elton John) and Gas Board (with Brian Ferry on guitar). In those days it was acceptable to rely upon a more primitive form of advertising and John Alpin of the J & J organisation would drive around Sunderland in a van with yellow taped lettering advertising his forthcoming attractions.

## The Ones That Got Away In ...

| | | |
|---|---|---|
| *Dear Mrs. Applebee* .............................. David Garrick | | *Forbidden Fruit* .................... The Nashville Teens |
| *Flowers On The Wall* ................... Adam, Mike & Tim | | *What'cha Gonna Do Now* ............. Chris Andrews |
| *I Struck It Rich* ............................................. Len Barry | | *Please Stay* .............................. The Cryin' Shames |
| *Younger Girl* ........................................... The Critters | | *All Strung Out* ......... Nino Tempo & April Stevens |

It was an unfortunate fact that Chris Andrews' formula songs began to loose their appeal before the lyrically clever *What'cha Gonna Do Now* was released and became a victim of the changing times.

Another of the year's releases to be sadly overlooked was *Flowers On The Wall* by Adam, Mike & Tim. The original version by the Statler Brothers made the higher echelons of the US charts. Neither the original recording nor the excellent British cover version drew breath over here.

*Please Stay* by The Cryin' Shames represented Joe Meek's finest hour. Tearful vocals and an outstanding production by Meek created an atmosphere record of unparalleled proportions. Management interest from Brian Epstein and a number two position on the Liverpool hit parade was to be the pinnacle of the group's success as they subsequently disappeared without trace.

South Shields' famous Cellar Club where
THE JUNCO PARTNERS and THE GAS BOARD
(featuring Brian Ferry) were regular visitors.

# In 1967 ...

Amen Corner made their chart debut with *Gin House Blues*.

Long John Baldry's first hit record *Let The Heartaches Begin* soared to the top of the charts.

The Beatles' double-sided record *Penny Lane/Strawberry Fields Forever* was their first single in twelve releases not to top the charts. It was held at number two by Engelbert Humperdinck's *Release Me*.

The Bee Gees scored their first chart hit with *New York Mining Disaster 1941* and their first number one with *Massachusetts* in April and September respectively.

Joe Brown scored a minor hit with a version of The Beatles' *With A Little Help From My Friends*.

At the height of 'flower power', The Flowerpot Men chalked up a one off hit with *Let's Go To San Francisco*.

Three top ten hits for Jimi Hendrix - *Hey Joe, Purple Haze* and *The Wind Cries Mary* - made this the best chart year for the highly rated guitarist/vocalist.

Pink Floyd released the singles *Arnold Layne* and *See Emily Play*.

The Royal Guardsmen were a surprise chart name thanks to the novelty record *Snoopy Vs. The Red Baron*.

## THE TREMELOES

Originally Brian Poole & The Tremeloes, the lead singer and backing group split in 1966 following a creditable run of four top ten hits. Against all predictions at the time, not only did The Tremeloes proceed to steal the limelight from their former lead singer but their subsequent chart successes eclipsed everything which they had collectively achieved in their former guise. An image re-structuring job saw the arrival of new front man Chip Hawkes, the donning of Carnaby Street clothes and the growing of the hair. The group signed to CBS Records and made soft harmony vocals their forte. Despite the pedigree of the first two songs to be released as singles, both *Blessed* (Paul Simon) and *Good Day Sunshine* (Lennon-McCartney) failed to sell. The next single, the Cat Stevens song *Here Comes My Baby*, gave The Trems their top ten breakthrough while the next single, *Silence Is Golden* (previously hidden away on the 'B' side of The Four Seasons' hit *Rag Doll*), climbed to the coveted number one position. A succession of hit singles followed, all bearing the familiar Tremeloes' hallmark. The songwriting teams which had been responsible for the hits up to mid-1969 were abandoned towards the end of the year as the group sought career expansion as composers of their own recordings. The first self-composed Tremeloes' release was *(Call Me) Number One* and it proved to be their strongest seller, just being kept from the number one spot by the year's biggest hit *Sugar Sugar* by The Archies. Illusions of grandeur may have been responsible for the group subsequently pressing the self destruct button when they became dismissive of their earlier hits and announced their intentions to 'progress' to heavy music. One hit later, The Tremeloes became a nostalgia act on the cabaret circuit!

**BIGGEST 1967 HIT : Silence Is Golden.**

**OTHER 60's CHART HITS INCLUDED :**
*Here Comes My Baby, Even The Bad Times Are Good, Suddenly You Love Me, Helule Helule, My Little Lady,
Hello World, (Call Me) Number One.*

# THE MOVE

Carly Wayne, Roy Wood, Trevor Burton, Chris Kefford and Bev Bevan were the nucleus of three of Birmingham's most popular beat groups of the mid sixties when they fused together early in 1966 to form The Move. The group re-located to London and soon secured a residency at the famed Marquee Club. Shortly afterwards the group were signed to Decca's new avant-garde Deram label which was the perfect vehicle for their inventive talents. The hits flowed immediately and together with some management initiated publicity stunts which optimised their outrageous behaviour, The Move became one of the highest profile groups of the late sixties. The musical content of the singles was as superb as it was varied; ranging from the classical inspiration of their first single *Night Of Fear* to the psychedelically influenced *I Can Hear The Grass Grow* to the out and out rock of *Brontosaurus*, each one was a carefully crafted three minute masterpiece. Their stage act involved antics which were not dissimilar to those of The Who; smashing cars and television sets and burning effigies of Adolf Hitler, Ian Smith et al. In September 1967 the group switched record labels to Regal Zonophone and the first release for the company, *Flowers In The Rain*, holds the dubious distinction of being the first ever record to be played on BBC Radio 1. The departure of Chris Kefford in 1968 reduced The Move to a four piece while a switch in the management brought further potential turmoil to the group who were, nevertheless, still charting on a regular basis thanks to the astute leadership of Roy Wood. As the decade drew to a close, differences of opinion within the group saw Carl Wayne attempt to divert the group towards the cabaret circuit in the wake of their unsuccessful U.S. concert tour. The culmination of the disagreements led to the departure of Wayne, leaving The Move to work as a trio until the recruitment of Jeff Lynne to the ranks in January 1970 whereupon the hits continued for a further two years.

> **BIGGEST 1967 HIT : Flowers In The Rain.**
>
> **OTHER 60's CHART HITS INCLUDED :**
> **Night Of Fear, I Can Hear The Grass Grow, Fire Brigade, Blackberry Way, Curly.**

## Wearside Top Ten ~ 9th February 1967

1. *I'm A Believer* ............................. The Monkees (RCA Victor)
2. *Matthew And Son* ................................... Cat Stevens (Deram)
3. *Night Of Fear* .......................................... The Move (Deram)
4. *I've Been A Bad Bad Boy* ......................... Paul Jones (HMV)
5. *Let's Spend The Night Together* ...............................
   The Rolling Stones (Decca)
6. *Standing In The Shadows Of Love* ..........................
   The Four Tops (Tamla Motown)
7. *Hey Joe* .............................................. Jimi Hendrix (Polydor)
8. *This Is My Song* ........................................ Petula Clark (Pye)
9. *Green Green Grass Of Home* .................. Tom Jones (Decca)
10. *Release Me* .......................... Engelbert Humperdinck (Decca)

## Wearside Top Ten ~ 13th April 1967

1. *Release Me* ........................ Engelbert Humperdinck (Decca)
2. *Somethin' Stupid* ............... Nancy & Frank Sinatra (Reprise)
3. *Puppet On A String* ..................................... Sandie Shaw (Pye)
4. *A Little Bit Me A Little Bit You* ... The Monkees (RCA Victor)
5. *Ha! Ha! Said The Clown* ............... Manfred Mann (Fontana)
6. *Simon Smith And The Amazing Dancing Bear* .....................
   Alan Price Set (Decca)
7. *Bernadette* .......................... The Four Tops (Tamla Motown)
8. *I Was Kaiser Bill's Batman* .... Whistling Jack Smith (Deram)
9. *Georgy Girl* ..................................... The Seekers (Columbia)
10. *Happy Together* .................................... The Turtles (London)

Cat Stevens made his top ten debut with *Matthew And Son*.

After eight years and twenty six charts hits with Decca, Billy Fury signed to Parlophone.

During the 'Summer Of Love', The Turtles struck twice with their west coast of America sound. *Happy Together* and *She'd Rather Be With Me* gave the group some richly deserved success.

**THE KINKS who enjoyed a run of eleven top ten singles between 1964 and 1967.**

# LULU

Lulu & The Luvvers arrived in London from Glasgow in 1964. The fifteen year old lead singer immediately shot to prominence with her revival of the old Isley Brothers number *Shout*, her rasping R & B vocals on that, her debut single, belieing her tender years. Subsequent releases sold poorly including a raucous version of *Here Comes The Night* (later a hit for Them) although her chart fortunes were restored with *Leave A Little Love*, a Les Reed song which Lulu placed second at the televised Brighton Song Festival in 1965. Being blessed with an easy going TV personality, Lulu began working as a solo performer as well as gigging with The Luvvers but in February 1966 she and the group parted company. After almost two years out of the hit parade Lulu left Decca for EMI's Columbia label where she was paired with in-vogue record producer Mickie Most. Their first collaboration, on a cover of Neil Diamond's *The Boat That I Row*, was an immediate hit. At this point Lulu's career really took off with further hit singles, a U.K. tour with The Beach Boys, phenomenal success in America (where her recording of *To Sir With Love* became a chart topper) and her own BBC TV variety show. Her highest chart placing came in 1969 with the Mickie Most production of *Boom Bang-A-Bang* which represented the U.K. in that year's Eurovision Song Contest. The song tied in first place with three others while climbing to second place on the charts. If it ain't broke don't fix it is a sound maxim but Lulu left Mickie Most and Columbia towards the end of 1969 and thereafter she struggled to re-capture her hit making form. A solitary hit after another label switch in the seventies and the re-issue of *Shout* in the eighties prior to her guest appearance on Take That's *Relight My Fire*, represented her only post Mickie Most chart successes.

> **BIGGEST 1967 HIT : The Boat That I Row.**
>
> **OTHER 60's CHART HITS INCLUDED :**
> *Shout, Leave A Little Love, Me The Peaceful Heart, I'm A Tiger, Boom Bang-A-Bang.*

## Wearside Top Ten ~ 22nd June 1967

1. A Whiter Shade Of Pale ..................... Procul Harum (Deram)
2. Carrie-Anne ................................. The Hollies (Parlophone)
3. There Goes My Everything ................................. Engelbert Humperdinck (Decca)
4. Waterloo Sunset ................................. The Kinks (Pye)
5. Silence Is Golden ................................. The Tremeloes (CBS)
6. The Happening ..................... The Supremes (Tamla Motown)
7. Okay ......... Dave Dee, Dozy, Beaky, Mick & Tich (Fontana)
8. Paper Sun ................................. Traffic (Island)
9. Then I Kissed Her ..................... The Beach Boys (Capitol)
10. Dedicated To The One I Love .................................. The Mamas & The Papas (RCA Victor)

## Wearside Top Ten ~ 16th August 1967

1. San Francisco (Be Sure To Wear Some Flowers In Your Hair) Scott McKenzie (CBS)
2. All You Need Is Love ..................... The Beatles (Parlophone)
3. Death Of A Clown ................................. Dave Davies (Pye)
4. I'll Never Fall In Love Again ................... Tom Jones (Decca)
5. I Was Made To Love Her ..... Stevie Wonder (Tamla Motown)
6. She'd Rather Be With Me ..................... The Turtles (London)
7. Up Up And Away .......... The Johnny Mann Singers (Liberty)
8. Even The Bad Times Are Good ........... The Tremeloes (CBS)
9. It Must Be Him ...................................... Vikki Carr (Liberty)
10. The House That Jack Built ................. Alan Price Set (Decca)

# THE MONKEES

Not a group for the serious student of pop but one which gave countless pleasure to their adoring fans. The Monkees were a manufactured pop phenomenon who, it was alleged, did not play on their early recordings and one which was assembled with personable males to win over a share of the lucrative female teen market which was lacking in ready made idols at that time. The original conception of the group was to create a sitcom around an American version of The Beatles and to that end an advertisement was placed in the Daily Variety newspaper. From the 437 hopefuls auditioned, the four successful applicants were Davy Jones (child actor), Mike Nesmith (musician), Peter Tork (folk singer) and Mickey Dolenz (child actor). The show, The Monkees, soon became popular with young teenagers initially in America and then in Britain where it made its BBC TV debut in January 1967. Simultaneously *I'm A Believer* was released as the group's second single (the first *Last Train To Clarksville*, initially flopped but later became a minor hit) and soared to the top of the charts with sales in excess of 750,000 while the LPs The *Monkees* and *More Of The Monkees* both topped the LP chart. Brill Building songwriters Carole King, Gerry Goffin, Neil Diamond and Neil Sedaka were hired to write material and the group were eventually given some artistic freedom to contribute to their record product. Three sell out concerts at Wembley's Empire Pool, a number one and a number two selling album and further top ten singles kept The Monkees' juggernaut in overdrive throughout 1967. A month is a long time in pop music and by early 1968 viewing figures for the television programme hit an all time low and record sales plummeted. The disastrous box office figures for the group's one and only big screen movie sealed their fate and by early 1969 The Monkees' demise was effectively complete. A phenomenally rapid rise to fame had been followed by one of the quickest career crashes of the decade.

> **BIGGEST 1967 HIT : I'm A Believer.**
>
> **OTHER 60's CHART HITS INCLUDED :**
> *A Little Bit Me A Little Bit You, Alternate Title, Pleasant Valley Sunday, Last Train To Clarksville, Daydream Believer.*

A young GENE PITNEY whose tenth and final top ten record of the decade was *Something's Gotten Hold Of My Heart* in 1967.

SANDIE SHAW
who won the 1967 Eurovision Song Contest for the United Kingdom with *Puppet On A String*. It was also the barefooted singer's third and final chart topper of the sixties.

There was a surprise chart comeback for Frankie Vaughan with his first single for Columbia, *There Must Be A Way*.

One of the decade's most memorable hits, *Excerpt From A Teenage Opera* by Keith West, was prevented from reaching number one by the less than memorable *The Last Waltz* by Engelbert Humperdinck.

*I Was Made To Love Her* became Stevie Wonder's first top ten chart hit.

Wetherells continued to rule the roost with a selection of star names never before seen in Sunderland. The first half of the year saw visits by the likes of Adam Faith, Wayne Fontana & The Mindbenders, Billy Fury, Mark Wynter and The Fortunes. Later in the year there were visits by The Moody Blues (before they attained the status of super stardom), American hit recording star Del Shannon, The Grumbleweeds and fifties rocker Marty Wilde.

Current hit makers to visit the Top Rank Suite included The Troggs and St. Louis Union.

Meanwhile, Wearside's Porama Club (which was situated above Jacksons The Tailors in High Street West) played host to Gerry & The Pacemakers, The Tornados, Freddie & The Dreamers, Billy J Kramer, Del Shannon and David & Jonathan. The first signs of a decline in Sunderland night life came with the news that the Porama Club was attracting as few as twelve people on some mid-week nights. The financial burden of providing meals, dancing and cabaret on nights when there were such poor attendances resulted in the club successfully applying for permission from Sunderland Licencing Court to close the lower ground floor of the premises.

Sunderland based CHRIS WARREN & THE STRANGERS whose interpretations of Cliff Richard material made them a popular act on the mid sixties club circuit. Chris Warren later experienced brief chart fame with Pickettywitch.

# THE BEE GEES

Barry, Maurice and Robin Gibb were born in the Isle of Man during the late forties but emigrated to Australia in 1958. A succession of Robin Gibb penned singles achieved commercial success down under but the brothers had aspirations of cracking the more lucrative British market and they returned to this country in 1967 where they landed a management contract with Robert Stigwood and a recording deal with Polydor. They enjoyed the luxury of having a chart hit with their first record - *New York Mining Disaster 1941* - with its unusual title and thought provoking lyrics but found the going tougher when their second single just managed to scrape into the top fifty chart. Throughout the late sixties The Bee Gees could take nothing for granted in the hit parade stakes with seemingly good commercial records failing to gain the recognition they deserved. The full extent of their seesaw chart career was apparent when the next single, *Massachusetts*, gave them their first number one record. Refusing to rest on their laurels they subsequently experimented with different musical styles as witnessed by the hits *World* and the beautifully laid back *Words*. The Bee Gees' double album *Odessa* represented the Gibbs' foray into psychedelia but the end result, although moderately successful in commercial terms, was not viewed as one of their greatest works. Following the disappointing sales of *Jumbo* the group enjoyed two further top ten hits and another relative flop before internal quarrels resulted in the departure of Robin (to pursue a solo career) and musicians Vince Melouney (guitar) and Colin Peterson (drums) leaving Barry and Maurice to continue as a duo. The act scored a solitary hit in that format, the MOR/Country flavoured *Don't Forget To Remember*. The Bee Gees sixties songwriting talents were recognised during the decade when *Only One Woman* by The Marbles charted (1968) as did Nina Simone's cover of the failed Bee Gees' single *To Love Somebody* (1969). The Gibb brothers were reconciled in 1972 and subsequently fulfilled their sixties potential as one of the most truly gifted and versatile groups to emerge from that swinging era.

> **BIGGEST 1967 HIT : Massachusetts.**
>
> **OTHER 60's CHART HITS INCLUDED :**
> *New York Mining Disaster 1941, World, Words, First Of May, I've Gotta Get A Message To You, Don't Forget To Remember.*

Further negative news came from the 'new style' Seaburn Hall which had been re-launched in a blaze of publicity with concerts planned with such names as The Kinks and Wayne Fontana & The Mindbenders. The venue was described in The Sunderland Echo as a "Ghost Ballroom" when only 100 people turned up to see The Kinks on 16th September. Worse was to follow on 23rd September when Wayne Fontana & The Mindbenders themselves failed to turn up. Chairman of Sunderland Seaside Development Committee said that although Sunderland Corporation had nothing to do with the organisation of these events - the organisers merely hired the hall - this sort of thing had cast a bad reflection upon Seaburn Hall. One problem was that there were no bar facilities for public events at Seaburn Hall and people preferred dancing at workingmen's clubs where they could drink. He thought that experiments of this sort might be more successful nearer Christmas.

It was in this year that the Dial A Disc service was launched. It was described as being a "swinging success" in Leeds where the exchange was handling over 50,000 calls per week. A different disc was played each day and chosen from the top seven best selling singles.

Back at the troubled Seaburn Hall, the venue which had first been opened by Sunderland Corporation in 1939, had become the subject of a discussion as to whether it should be handed over to private enterprise.

## Wearside Top Ten ~ 25th October 1967

1. *Massachusetts* ..................................... The Bee Gees (Polydor)
2. *Hole In My Shoe* ..................................... Traffic (Island)
3. *The Last Waltz* ..................... Engelbert Humperdinck (Decca)
4. *Flowers In The Rain* ............... The Move (Regal Zonophone)
5. *Baby Now That I've Found You* ......... The Foundations (Pye)
6. *Zabadak* ..... Dave Dee, Dozy, Beaky, Mick & Tich (Fontana)
7. *The Letter* ..................................... The Box Tops (Stateside)
8. *Homburg* ........................... Procul Harum (Regal Zonophone)
9. *From The Underworld* ........................... The Herd (Fontana)
10. *Excerpt From A Teenage Opera* ..... Keith West (Parlophone)

## Wearside Top Ten ~ 27th December 1967

1. *Hello Goodbye* ............................. The Beatles (Parlophone)
2. *Magical Mystery Tour (EP)* ........... The Beatles (Parlophone)
3. *If The Whole World Stopped Loving* ....... Val Doonican (Pye)
4. *Something's Gotten Hold Of My Heart* ...................................
   Gene Pitney (Stateside)
5. *Daydream Believer* ..................... The Monkees (RCA Victor)
6. *I'm Coming Home* ................................. Tom Jones (Decca)
7. *All My Love* ..................................... Cliff Richard (Columbia)
8. *Let The Heartaches Begin* ............... Long John Baldry (Pye)
9. *Walk Away Renee* ................ The Four Tops (Tamla Motown)
10. *Kites* ............. Simon Dupree & The Big Sound (Parlophone)

# THE FOUNDATIONS

Pop/Soul group The Foundations were formed in early 1967 and were probably the most cosmopolitan singles chart outfit of the decade. Trinidad, Jamaica, England, Dominica and Sri Lanka were the global areas represented in the group which also encompassed a wide spectrum of ages. The Foundations first came to the attention of a London record dealer as they rehearsed in a local club and an introduction to hit songwriters Tony Macauley and John MacLeod resulted in the release of the group's first record, the opus pop/soul classic *Baby Now That I've Found You* which topped the British charts and became a top ten hit in America while clocking up worldwide sales of three million in the process. Two less successful singles followed before before the second multi-million seller came along in the shape of the Mike D'Abo (of Manfred Mann fame)/Tony Macauley song *Build Me Up Buttercup*. This infectious piece of commercial pop restored the group's flagging chart fortunes and despite the subsequent untimely departure of lead singer Clem Curtis to pursue a solo career, The Foundations made a brisk chart return with the more melodic *In The Bad Bad Old Days* which produced the group's third top ten entry in eighteen months. Following the departure of Curtis, saxophonist Mike Elliott left the group and internal bickerings led to the break up of The Foundations immediately after the failure of their September 1969 release *Born To Live And Born To Die*. The Foundations' name was later resurrected in two derivative forms, one of which toured during the nineties as Clem Curtis & The Foundations.

**BIGGEST 1967 HIT : Baby Now That I've Found You.**

**OTHER 60's CHART HITS INCLUDED :**
**Back On My Feet Again, Build Me Up Buttercup, In The Bad Bad Old Days.**

The Chairman of Sunderland Seaside Development Committee said that Seaburn Hall had been losing money for the past two years and that the council could no longer afford to run it. It was proposed to advertise the venue to see if any offers were forthcoming to run the building as a commercial concern. Within five weeks of that advertisement, Wharton Entertainments expressed an interest in leasing the hall for £3,500 per year for the "development of catering facilities and the promotion of dances, shows and occasional wrestling contests". Some Councillors asked for assurances that bingo would not be played and that Sunderland would not become a Las Vegas.

In early 1967 THE SPENCER DAVIS GROUP hit the top ten charts for the fourth and final time with *I'm A Man*.

# *The Ones That Got Away In ...*

| | |
|---|---|
| *You've Not Changed* ............................ Sandie Shaw | *Best Part Of Breaking Up* ............... The Symbols |
| *Birds And Bees* ..................................... Warm Sounds | *Girl You'll Be A Woman Soon* ........ Neil Diamond |
| *To Love Somebody* ............................... The Bee Gees | *24 Sycamore* ................................... Wayne Fontana |
| *Tell It To The Rain* .......................... The Four Seasons | *Run To The Door* .............................. Clinton Ford |
| *Suzanne In The Mirror* ............................... Billy Fury | |

The Symbols' *Best Part Of Breaking Up* was a cover of The Ronettes' 1964 minor hit and seemed destined for a high chart placing when it suddenly nosedived from a number twenty five peak.

*Birds And Bees* by Warm Sounds was one of the earliest releases on the then fledgling Deram record label. The catchy close harmonies and strong promotional support by the parent Decca Record Company failed to muster sufficient sales to secure the anticipated high chart placing.

Billy Fury's label switch from Decca to Parlophone coincided with an immediate downturn in the singer's chart fortunes. *Suzanne In The Mirror* was Fury's third single on Parlophone and was unquestionably one of the year's finest releases. Its production was way ahead of its time and different from anything which Britain's best every male vocalist had attempted in the past. The mediocre sales of *Suzanne In The Mirror* was the low point of the year.

Clinton Ford's *Run To The Door* was an ultra catchy piece of country pop which stood on the threshold of top twenty chart honours for three months but inexplicably failed to rise higher than number twenty five position.

*WINING *DINING *DANCING *CABARET

## Porama

### Sunderland's Latest NIGHT CLUB
ABOVE JACKSONS THE TAILORS

**CABARET WEEK COMMENCING JANUARY 14th**

Early: DAVE SWANN
Late: STARLITES
Dancing to the Eric Carrol Trio
**TUESDAY NIGHT IS LADIES' LUCKY DRAW NIGHT**

| French Roulette, Dice & Blackjack played nightly | Memberships available — 10/6 single £1/1/0 double | Book Your Social Function Now |

*The Porama Club was one of several night clubs in Sunderland during the sixties.*

## In 1968 ...

The Beatles released their last Parlophone single of the decade (*Lady Madonna*) and their first on the Apple label (*Hey Jude*).

Instrumentalist Herb Alpert climbed the chart with his only U.K. vocal hit, *This Guy's In Love With You.*

The Casuals were one of the year's chart newcomers when *Jesamine* was kept from the coveted number one spot by Mary Hopkin's *Those Were The Days.*

## LOVE AFFAIR

Fronted by the charismatic Steve Ellis, Love Affair were formed in 1966 and performed on a semi-professional basis for three years. A chance recording of the Robert Knight song *Everlasting Love* by Ellis and some session musicians was released by CBS Records and took everyone by surprise when it began to climb the charts during the first week of 1968. Within four weeks it had secured top spot and Love Affair were hastily knocked into shape as a full time professional act, managed by drummer Mo Bacon's father. The decision to resist the overtures of the major players in the music business probably cost the group dearly as they failed to fully exploit their potential and their meteoric rise to fame was to be short lived. Following the chart topping success of *Everlasting Love,* the group and Ellis in particular, with his face on the cover of every teen magazine, became instant idols of the female teenage fraternity. A further four chart hits in fifteen months followed before Steve Ellis left the group to form his own line up. Keyboard player Morgan Fisher also departed and later appeared in Mott The Hoople. Love Affair was such a well known name during the late sixties that it is surprising to reflect upon the fact that their chart life lasted a mere nineteen months, although it was a concentrated period of success with five hits spanning fifty six chart weeks of the seventy six calendar weeks.

**BIGGEST 1968 HIT : *Everlasting Love.***

**OTHER 60's CHART HITS INCLUDED :**
***Rainbow Valley, A Day Without Love, One Road, Bringing On Back The Good Times.***

### Top Rank SUITE

— Tuesday, 27th August —
We Present A Fantastic Night Out With

# The Small Faces
And
THE TOBY TWIRL
Also
D.J. Mike Powell
Advance Tickets Now On Sale 10/-.   7.00—11.00

**Top Rank SUNDERLAND SUITE**
Park Lane. Tel:- Sunderland 59548

*ABOVE*
**TOBY TWIRL** had a strong following at Wetherells Club particularly on their 'half crown' nights. Here they supported SMALL FACES just around the corner from Wetherells at Top Rank Suite in Sunderland.

*RIGHT*
**The wonderful BILLY FURY at Club Latino in 1968.**

STAR-TIME AT THE

## LATiNO
CROSSGATE   •   SOUTH SHIELDS
TEL: 2581   •   OPEN FROM   7. PM

**TONIGHT & ALL THIS WEEK**
*Wining, Dining, Dancing and Cabaret*

Cabaret at 10 p.m.
'Top of the Pops'
Singer/Recording Star

# BILLY FURY

8 p.m.: Continental Speciality Magician
**WEYGANDA**

Midnight
The exciting talent of the Singer with the Big Voice
**BERYL BRYDEN**

*No cover charge to members except Friday, Saturday*

A BAILEY NIGHT-SPOT!

56

## Wearside Top Ten ~ 3rd February 1968

1. *Everlasting Love* ....................... Love Affair (CBS)

2. *Am I That Easy To Forget* ... Engelbert Humperdinck (Decca)

3. *Judy In Disguise (With Glasses)* ..................................
   John Fred & The Playboy Band (Pye International)

4. *Ballad Of Bonnie And Clyde* ........ Georgie Fame (Columbia)

5. *Mighty Quinn* ................................. Manfred Mann (Fontana)

6. *She Wears My Ring* ..................... Solomon King (Columbia)

7. *Bend Me Shape Me* ............................ Amen Corner (Deram)

8. *Suddenly You Love Me* ......................... The Tremeloes (CBS)

9. *Everything I Am* ............................ Plastic Penny (Page One)

10. *Daydream Believer* ..................... The Monkees (RCA Victor)

## Wearside Top Ten ~ 10th April 1968

1. *Congratulations* ............................. Cliff Richard (Columbia)

2. *Lady Madonna* ............................. The Beatles (Parlophone)

3. *Delilah* ..................................... Tom Jones (Decca)

4. *What A Wonderful World* ............... Louis Armstrong (HMV)

5. *(Sittin' On) The Dock Of The Bay* .......... Otis Reading (Stax)

6. *If I Only Had Time* ................................ John Rowles (MCA)

7. *Simon Says* ............................ 1910 Fruitgum Company (Pye)

8. *Jennifer Eccles* ............................. The Hollies (Parlophone)

9. *If I Were A Carpenter* ......... The Four Tops (Tamla Motown)

10. *Step Inside Love* ............................. Cilla Black (Columbia)

## STATUS QUO

Status Quo were born in November 1967 while the embryonic version, The Spectres, were first conceived in 1962. They began playing at workingmen's clubs in 1964 and by the following year they had won a four month contract with Butlin's. In 1965 The Spectres signed to Piccadilly Records (an offshoot of Pye) and after three unsuccessful singles changed their name to Traffic Jam. Enter Rick Parfitt, a second name change and a new record deal with the mainstream Pye Records. Status Quo's first release was *Pictures Of Matchstick Men* and caught everyone by surprise when it climbed the charts to a respectable seventh position. At the time the group were working as Madeline Bell's backing band and were still managed on a part-time basis! The next single *Black Veils of Melancholy* failed to stir record buyers into action as did their debut LP *Picturesque Matchstickable Messages*. The tracks on the LP showed the group to be completely devoid of musical direction and contained a contrived mixture of songs; three examples being *Spicks And Specks* (Bee Gees), *Sheila* (Tommy Roe) and *Green Tambourine* (Lemon Pipers). *Ice In The Sun* put the group firmly back into the charts during the late summer of 1968 and the group were temporarily given a chic image. It may have been the new image which landed them a guest spot on Gene Pitney's U.K. tour the following year as an out and out pop group. The ballad *Are You Growing Tired Of My Love* was chosen as the single to tie in with the tour and it deserved much better than its final mediocre chart placing. When Quo's second album failed to sell, the band decided to change their image and musical direction. The twelve bar metamorphosis was about to take shape.

**BIGGEST 1968 HIT : Pictures Of Matchstick Men.**

**OTHER 60's CHART HITS INCLUDED :**
*Ice In The Sun, Are You Growing Tired Of My Love.*

JETHRO TULL
in Billingham during 1968,
one year prior to cracking the
charts with *Living In The Past*.

*Keep On* restored Bruce Channel to the charts after a six year absence.

EMI Records discontinued its HMV label.

The Swinging Blue Jeans announced their split when group member Terry Sylvester left to join The Hollies.

Dave Dee, Dozy, Beaky, Mick & Tich celebrated having a number one hit with *The Legend Of Xanadu*. Despite having eight top ten hits this was their only chart topper.

Chart debutant Johnny Nash had the first of three hits in the sixties with *Hold Me Tight*.

## CLUB FIESTA

SUNDAY, OCTOBER 20 FOR SEVEN DAYS
# THE KINKS
PAUL MELBA ● ROSA ROBERTS
NORTON ROAD, STOCKTON-on-TEES. Tel. 53046

## CLUB FIESTA

MONDAY ONLY, SEPTEMBER 9
### CLIFF RICHARD
Appearing in separate shows at 8 p.m and 11-30 p.m.
TUESDAY — SATURDAY
### DICKIE VALENTINE
Appearing at 11-30 nightly
NORTON ROAD, STOCKTON-on-TEES. Tel. 53046

*ABOVE*
**The stature of the Fiesta Club in Stockton during the late sixties was immense.
THE KINKS and CLIFF RICHARD were just two of the big name acts to appear at the
popular night spot in 1968.**

*BELOW*
Vocalist/guitarist JIMI HENDRIX who scored
three top ten hits in 1967 and a solitary top ten
success in 1968; *All Along The Watchtower.*

Thirteen top ten records including three number ones made MANFRED MANN
into a household name from 1964 until the end of the decade.
*Mighty Quinn* topped the charts in 1968.

# MANFRED MANN

One of the most enduring chart acts of the sixties, Manfred Mann's early distinctive sound relied heavily upon Paul Jones' vibrant R & B vocals and prominent harmonica playing. By January 1964 the group consisted of Jones, Manfred Mann, Mike Vickers, Tom McGuinness and Mike Hugg and had already released two singles on HMV when they were invited to write the new theme music for TV pop show Ready Steady Go. The result was the unforgettable *5-4-3-2-1* which also gave them their first chart hit and paved the way for an impressive run of Paul Jones fronted hits over the next two years. These included two number ones; *Do Wah Diddy Diddy* and *Pretty Flamingo*. Such was the popularity of the group during the mid sixties that *The One In The Middle* four track EP sold strongly enough to make number six on the singles chart. Having given twelve months' notice of his intention to leave the group to pursue a solo career, Paul Jones left Manfred Mann in July 1966 at the height of their popularity and with *Pretty Flamingo* perched at number one. At that time, the departure of a group's lead vocalist inevitably signalled the end of their chart fortunes. Curiously, a switch of record label also often had an adverse effect on record sales. Paul Jones was replaced by Mike D'Abo (in preference to Rod Stewart, Wayne Fontana and Long John Baldry), Mike Vickers was replaced by Jack Bruce and the group moved from HMV to Fontana. D'Abo fitted the group like a glove and the hit making formula continued on Fontana without the slightest interruption. While Jones sang lead vocal on six of Manfred Mann's top ten hits, D'Abo sang on seven. January 1968 saw the group back at the top of the charts with Dylan's *Mighty Quinn* (the third Bob Dylan song to have been taken into the top ten by Manfred Mann) and the comment from the man himself that he regarded the group to be the best interpreters of his songs. The outfit ended the decade with an impressive collection of hits before making the decision to open a new chapter of their career by playing the jazz and blues based numbers which had always been prevalent on their sixties LPs. Mann later formed Manfred Mann's Earth Band in 1973.

**BIGGEST 1968 HIT : *Mighty Quinn.***
**OTHER 60's CHART HITS INCLUDED :**
*5-4-3-2-1, Do Wah Diddy Diddy, Sha La La, Come Tomorrow, If You Gotta Go Go Now, Pretty Flamingo,
Ha Ha Said The Clown, Semi Detached Suburban Mr. James, Fox On The Run.*

## Wearside Top Ten ~ 12th June 1968

1. *Young Girl* ..................... The Union Gap (CBS)
2. *Jumping Jack Flash* ................... The Rolling Stones (Decca)
3. *A Man Without Love* .......... Engelbert Humperdinck (Decca)
4. *Honey* ........................ Bobby Goldsboro (United Artists)
5. *Rainbow Valley* ............................... Love Affair (CBS)
6. *This Wheel's On Fire* ............................................. Julie Driscoll, Brian Auger & The Trinity (Marmalade)
7. *Blue Eyes* ............................. Don Partridge (Columbia)
8. *Hurdy Gurdy Man* ................................ Donovan (Pye)
9. *Do You Know The Way To San Jose* .. Dionne Warwick (Pye)
10. *I Don't Want Our Loving To Die* ............ The Herd (Fontana)

## Wearside Top Ten ~ 21st August 1968

1. *Fire* .................... The Crazy World Of Arthur Brown (Track)
2. *Mony Mony* ....................................................... Tommy James & The Shondells (Major Minor)
3. *Do It Again* ..................... The Beach Boys (Capitol)
4. *This Guy's In Love With You* ................ Herb Alpert (A & M)
5. *I Close My Eyes And Count To Ten* ............................... Dusty Springfield (Philips)
6. *Help Yourself* ............................. Tom Jones (Decca)
7. *Sunshine Girl* ......................... Herman's Hermits (Columbia)
8. *I've Gotta Get A Message To You* .... The Bee Gees (Polydor)
9. *Mrs. Robinson* ............................ Simon & Garfunkel (CBS)
10. *High In The Sky* ................................. Amen Corner (Deram)

# HERMAN'S HERMITS

Fronted by Peter Noone, Herman's Hermits first came to the attention of record producer Mickie Most in 1964 when, recognising the huge potential of the act, he signed the group to an exclusive production deal. Simultaneously, Most secured the group a recording contract with Columbia Records. Their debut release was a revival of Earl Jean's U.S. hit *I'm Into Something Good*. It was released during August 1964 and became an instant hit, topping the charts by September and becoming the forerunner of a string of sixties hits not only in Britain but also in America where they became an even bigger name with sales of over ten million records in 1965. Most of the group's hits consisted of Noone's vocals backed by session musicians (including Jimmy Page and John Paul Jones, later of Led Zeppelin fame) with Mickie Most producing. Almost uniquely, the group appealed strongly to an older generation at the same time as causing mass hysteria in their role of teen idols. Revivals of fifties U.S. hits such as *Silhouettes* and *Wonderful World* maintained the high chart profile of the group throughout 1965 at a time when they were absent from these shores on a marathon American tour. In America they successfully released the U.K. chart material as well as breaking into vaudeville with *Mrs. Brown You've Got A Lovely Daughter* and *I'm Henry VIII I Am* both of which became chart toppers without even being considered for British release due to the banality of the lyrics. By 1966 the stature of the group was such that they had access to material written by the leading songwriters of the day; Graham Gouldman and Ray Davies being just two of the respected names to pen Herman's Hermits hits. A British tour with The Fortunes, Billy Fury and Wayne Fontana & The Mindbenders was hugely successful and coupled with their canny knack of releasing infectious, catchy material on record, their star continued to shine brightly right through until the beginning of the seventies by which time the appeal of the formula songs started to wear thin. Noone and the group split in December 1970 after one of the most successful chart runs of the entire sixties.

**BIGGEST 1968 HIT : Something's Happening.**

**OTHER 60's CHART HITS INCLUDED :**
*I'm Into Something Good, Silhouettes, Wonderful World, A Must To Avoid, No Milk Today,*
*There's A Kind Of Hush, Sunshine Girl, My Sentimental Friend.*

Busker Don Partridge became an overnight success when *Rosie* and *Blue Eyes* brought him fame and fortune.

Otis Redding had his one and only top ten hit with *(Sittin' On) The Dock Of The Bay.*

After just missing out on top ten honours throughout the mid sixties with brother Paul, Barry Ryan hit the number two spot with *Eloise.*

Andy Williams released his third and final top ten hit of the decade; *Can't Take My Eyes Off You.*

The only chart hit for Crazy World Of Arthur Brown, *Fire,* hit top spot.

# MARMALADE

This no frills unashamedly commercial pop group paid their dues in Glasgow's clubland as Dean Ford & The Gaylords for six years from 1961. They made the move to London with a line up which consisted of four Glaswegians plus Shropshire born drummer Alan Whitehead and changed their name to Marmalade. After four unsuccessful singles as the Gaylords with Norrie Paramor at Columbia, the newly named group joined CBS. Live work at this time was nothing more than supporting appearances on concert tours and the occasional ballroom spots playing cover versions of current chart hits. After three disappointing singles on CBS, Marmalade finally hit the big time with a catchy cover of The Grass Roots' *Lovin' Things* and quickly followed it up with the equally commercial but rather less successful *Wait For Me Marianne*. They seized upon The Beatles' *White Album* as soon as it was released and hurriedly recorded their version of *Ob-La-Di Ob-La-Da* which was arguably the most commercial track on the album. The ploy worked to perfection as the single rose to the summit of the hit parade to give Marmalade their only number one hit. The ballad *Baby Make It Soon* gave them their final chart hit on CBS before their defection to the Decca label in a deal which guaranteed total artistic control over their recorded output. The freedom from record company interference worked well as Marmalade hit the top ten four times during their time with Decca although apart from the December 1969 chart entry of *Reflections Of My Life* all four singles enjoyed their moments of chart glory during the seventies.

> **BIGGEST 1968 HIT : Ob-La-Di Ob-La-Da.**
>
> **OTHER 60's CHART HITS INCLUDED :**
> *Lovin' Things, Wait For Me Marianne, Baby Make It Soon, Reflections Of My Life.*

## Wearside Top Ten ~ 9th October 1968

1. *Those Were The Days* .......................... Mary Hopkin (Apple)
2. *Jesamine* ................................ The Casuals (Decca)
3. *Hey Jude* ................................ The Beatles (Apple)
4. *Little Arrows* ............................... Leapy Lee (MCA)
5. *My Little Lady* ...................................... The Tremeloes (CBS)
6. *Lady Willpower* ................................. The Union Gap (CBS)
7. *Ice In The Sun* ............................... Status Quo (Pye)
8. *Red Balloon* ....................... The Dave Clark Five (Columbia)
9. *Hold Me Tight* ................... Johnny Nash (Regal Zonophone)
10. *I Say A Little Prayer* ..................... Aretha Franklin (Atlantic)

## Wearside Top Ten ~ 11th December 1968

1. *The Good, The Bad & The Ugly* ...............................................
   Hugo Montenegro (RCA Victor)
2. *Lily The Pink* ................................ The Scaffold (Parlophone)
3. *Ain't Got No - I Got Life* ....................... Nina Simone (RCA)
4. *Build Me Up Buttercup* ..................... The Foundations (Pye)
5. *Eloise* ...................................... Barry Ryan (MGM)
6. *I'm The Urban Spaceman* ......................................................
   The Bonzo Dog Doo-Dah Band (Liberty)
7. *This Old Heart Of Mine* ........................................................
   The Isley Brothers (Tamla Motown)
8. *Breaking Down The Walls Of Heartache* ...............................
   Johnny Johnson & The Bandwagon (Direction)
9. *May I Have The Next Dream With You* ..................................
   Malcolm Roberts (Major Minor)
10. *I'm A Tiger* ...................................... Lulu (Columbia)

A significant development in Sunderland nightlife was the inroads which The Bay Hotel was starting to make into the pop market. These inroads were to pave the way for a joint venture with the Fillmore organisation during the following year. Two groups which were to play at The Bay Hotel were Plastic Penny (whose line-up contained local members) and St. Louise Union. Also in Sunderland, activity over at the Top Rank Suite in a three month spell between early August and early November included eight top rated shows. Names headlining these shows were Plastic Penny, Small Faces, Love Affair, Status Quo, Wayne Fontana & The Mindbenders, The Casuals, Dave Dee, Dozy, Beaky, Mick & Tich and the return of Love Affair. 28th November saw the grand opening of Annabel Club which was described as the 'North East's Most Exciting New Club Discotheque'. Names booked for the first few weeks included Cliff Bennett & The Rebel Rousers, Chris Farlowe, The Flirtations and Marmalade.

**THE MOVE whose recorded output of the late sixties made them one of the top names of the day.**

# THE DAVE CLARK FIVE

Tottenham's answer to Liverpool, The Dave Clark Five existed in various embryonic formations prior to the one comprising Dave Clark, Mike Smith, Lenny Davidson, Dennis Payton and Rick Huxley which signed to Columbia Records in February 1963. After a flop and a minor hit the group recorded *Glad All Over* which, like most of the subsequent hits, was written by Dave Clark and Mike Smith and bore all the DC5 traits of Clark's unsophisticated thumping drum sound and Smith's hoarse vocals. When the record displaced The Beatles' *I Want To Hold Your Hand* from the top of the U.K. charts the tabloid press had a field day with outrageous headlines. In reality Dave Clark & Co were no threat to The Beatles or to their crown as beat group leaders and after that initial chart topper they scored with their two immediate follow-ups *Bits And Pieces* (number two) and *Can't You See That She's Mine* (number ten) before missing the top twenty completely with their next four releases. While they struggled to fullfil their early promise in Britain, they could do no wrong in America with a veritable string of chart hits where their fans were slower to abandon their appreciation of the group's predictable formula sound than were their transatlantic cousins. The group spent more and more time in America with hectic touring schedules and television work while the summer of 1964 saw U.S. financial backing for the DC5's debut film *Catch Us If You Can*. The film yielded a first U.K. hit in fourteen months when the title track hit the top five but the outfit's erratic chart form returned when their next single *Over And Over* stalled at number forty five in Britain while topping the American charts. Three further top ten hits during the decade gave a fact file of seven top ten hits including a solitary number one between November 1963 and December 1969 which was creditable but hardly Beatle threatening!

Louis Armstrong became the decade's oldest chart topper when *What A Wonderful World* hit number one.

Joe Cocker became the fourth artist to hit top spot with a cover of a Beatles' song when *With A Little Help From My Friends* rose to pole position. The other artists to take a Beatles' song to number one were Billy J. Kramer & The Dakotas *(Bad To Me)*, Peter & Gordon *(World Without Love)* and The Overlanders *(Michelle)*. Marmalade subsequently repeated the achievement in 1969 with *Ob-La-Di Ob-La-Da.*

# *The Ones That Got Away In ...*

Sound Asleep ................................................... The Turtles
Rudi's In Love ................................................ The Locomotive
What Have They Done To Hazel ........... Ray Ennis & The Blue Jeans
I'm In A Different World ................................ The Four Tops
Honey Chile .................................. Martha & The Vandellas
I Shall Be Released ....................................... The Tremeloes
It's Your Day Today ............................................ P.J. Proby

California based group The Turtles are forever recorded in the annals of pop history as the purveyors of three classic pieces of mid sixties pop - *Happy Together, She'd Rather Be With Me* and *Eleanor* - although they deserved so much more. Several of their U.S. hits were sadly overlooked in this country and their first self-produced single, *Sound Asleep,* was one of the year's best releases but sold poorly.

*Rudi's In Love* by The Locomotive was a memorable turntable hit and it is now surprising to reflect upon the fact that this ska flavoured chunk of late sixties pop failed to break into the top twenty charts of the day.

1963/64 represented The Swinging Blue Jeans' heyday as a chart act. Despite releasing some creditable singles in later years, their recording career hit a downward path soon after the initial clutch of hits. In an attempt to re-define the group's image *What Have They Done To Hazel* was credited to Ray Ennis & The Blue Jeans but saleswise it failed miserably.

Sixties style advertising for the highly fashionable Chelsea Cat discotheque.

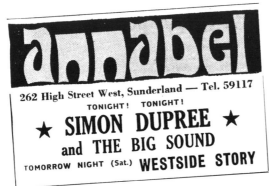

SIMON DUPREE & THE BIG SOUND created a classic sixties hit in 1967 with *Kites*. By 1969 they were working the night club circuit and played a date at Annabel in Sunderland.

# In 1969 ...

*The Ballad Of John & Yoko* became the fifth Beatles' hit single to contain a girl's name in the title.

*Sugar Sugar* by The Archies was the year's biggest seller with eight weeks at number one.

David Bowie made his chart debut with *Space Oddity*.

Radio One banned *Je T'Aime --- Moi Non Plus* by Jane Birkin & Serge Gainsbourg and in doing so catapulted the single to pole position in the process. A more acceptable version of the number *Love At First Sight* by Sounds Nice was played by the BBC but was only a minor chart hit.

Regular seventies hit maker Glen Campbell had his first taste of chart glory on the tiny Ember record label with *Wichita Lineman* and *Galveston*.

Reggae ruled when *The Israelites* by Desmond Dekker & The Aces topped the charts.

*The Way It Used To Be* made it seven straight top five hits for Engelbert Humperdinck.

Jethro Tull became a top ten debutant with *Living In The Past*.

## THE WHO

The Who were first launched on the back of the Mod movement in 1964. The group successfully developed an anti-social reputation and a notoriety for smashing up their instruments on stage. A regular Tuesday night spot at The Marquee Club introduced them to a wider audience but despite this they were unable to land a recording contract, partly due to their well publicised violent behaviour. Eventually they made it on to vinyl via a circuitous route; signing to American Decca who, in turn, leased their recordings to Brunswick for U.K. release. Ironically Brunswick records were marketed in the U.K. by Decca (who had earlier rejected the group!). The Who's first record the Kinks' inspired *I Can't Explain,* was mellow by comparison with the group's live reputation but the follow-up to that hit answered the call of those expecting an explosive performance on record; *Anyway Anyhow Anywhere* being unlike anything that the charts has seen at that time. With Pete Townsend now established as the group's composer, mid sixties chart output came thick and fast; contractual wranglings dictating a transient record label scenario with Brunswick, Reaction and Track all handling the group's recordings. Various staged managed publicity stunts and outrageous press quotes helped to maintain a high profile while the lyrical subject matter of the singles was as varied as it was risqué. Transvestism (*I'm A Boy*) and masturbation (*Pictures Of Lily*) were just two of the subjects dealt with on mid sixties Who recordings. The Who's major LP project of the sixties was the double LP release of Tommy, the rock opera about the deaf dumb and blind boy who excelled at playing pinball. The single *Pinball Wizard* gave the group their ninth top ten chart hit and their last of the decade. The Who rounded off the sixties in style with a blockbuster performance at Woodstock, an appearance with Bob Dylan at the Isle Of Wight Festival and a tour of European opera houses performing Tommy.

**BIGGEST 1969 HIT : Pinball Wizard.**

**OTHER 60's CHART HITS INCLUDED :**
*I Can't Explain, My Generation, Substitute, I'm A Boy, Happy Jack, I Can See For Miles.*

# CREEDENCE CLEARWATER REVIVAL

John Fogerty, Tom Fogerty, Stu Cook and Doug 'Cosmo' Clifford first began playing together in 1964 on a semi-professional basis, initially as The Blue Velvets and later as The Golliwogs (apparently to identify themselves with the British invasion!). In December 1967 they became Creedence Clearwater Revival and soon found themselves categorised by the rock press as a post psychedelic American group. CCR's debut single about a Mississippi steamboat was composed by lead singer John Fogerty and was an immediate hit. *Proud Mary* later became the group's most covered song with notable recorded versions by The Checkmates, Elvis Presley and Ike & Tina Turner. The next U.K. single was *Bad Moon Rising* and topped the chart during the summer of 1969 and in doing so established Creedence Clearwater Revival as a major force in Britain with an impressive run of hits, most of which charted during the seventies and as such are out of the scope of this book. By the end of the decade they were recognised as being America's premier working group blending the characteristic CCR sound with thoughtful, often socially aware lyrics. As is so often the case, upon the realisation of super-stardom, the group pressed the self destruct button in the early seventies as internal relationships, particularly between the Fogerty brothers, led to the reduction of the line up to a trio which in turn resulted in a rapid decline in chart fortunes. The group finally split in 1972.

**BIGGEST 1969 HIT : Bad Moon Rising.**

**OTHER 60's CHART HITS INCLUDED :**
**Proud Mary, Green River.**

## Wearside Top Ten ~ 11th January 1969

1. Ob-La-Di Ob-La-Da ................................ Marmalade (CBS)
2. Lily The Pink ............................. The Scaffold (Parlophone)
3. Build Me Up Buttercup .................... The Foundations (Pye)
4. I'm The Urban Spaceman ......................................................
   The Bonzo Dog Doo-Dah Band (Liberty)
5. Albatross ............................. Fleetwood Mac (Blue Horizon)
6. Sabre Dance ........................... Love Sculpture (Parlophone)
7. Something's Happening ......... Herman's Hermits (Columbia)
8. For Once In My Life .......... Stevie Wonder (Tamla Motown)
9. Ain't Got No - I Got Life ...................... Nina Simone (RCA)
10. Son Of A Preacher Man .............. Dusty Springfield (Philips)

## Wearside Top Ten ~ 22nd February 1969

1. (If Paradise Is) Half As Nice ....... Amen Corner (Immediate)
2. Blackberry Way ..................... The Move (Regal Zonophone)
3. Where Do You Go To My Lovely ...............................................
   ..........................................................Peter Sarstedt (United Artists)
4. I'm Gonna Make You Love Me ........................Diana Ross &
   The Supremes & The Temptations (Tamla Motown)
5. Dancing In The Street ...........................................................
   Martha Reeves & The Vandellas (Tamla Motown)
6. Albatross ............................. Fleetwood Mac (Blue Horizon)
7. You Got Soul ........................... Johnny Nash (Major Minor)
8. For Once In My Life .......... Stevie Wonder (Tamla Motown)
9. Please Don't Go ........................... Donald Peers (Columbia)
10. To Love Somebody ................................ Nina Simone (RCA)

# AMEN CORNER

Signed to the then highly fashionable Deram record label, Amen Corner were formed in Cardiff in 1966 where they built a reputation as one of the country's best live R & B groups. The out and out blues sound of their debut chart hit *Gin House Blues* further reinforced their high profile with the British R & B fraternity. Almost overnight, lead singer Andy Fairweather-Low emerged as a pin-up star and the group's sound was changed to accommodate more commercial pop material. The sax orientated dance single *Bend Me Shape Me* introduced Amen Corner to a new wider market as the group abandoned their R & B roots on a string of successful pop singles in their search for crossover fame and fortune. In 1969, Amen Corner followed the path which Small Faces had taken two years earlier when they left the Decca organisation to sign for Andrew Oldham's Immediate label. Their first outing on Immediate (*If Paradise Is) Half As Nice,* was an outstanding success and one of the fastest moving singles to the coveted number one spot during the entire decade. The follow-up, *Hello Suzie,* continued in the same vein as its predecessor and unexpectedly gave the group its final chart hit. The next record was a curious re-make of *Get Back* (which had been a hit for The Beatles a mere seven months earlier) but the release coincided with the closure of Immediate Records as a result of financial problems and accordingly it received no promotional backing. At this point Amen Corner ceased to be although Andy Fairweather-Low and four of the six other group members re-united to form Fair Weather.

**BIGGEST 1969 HIT : (If Paradise Is) Half As Nice.**

**OTHER 60's CHART HITS INCLUDED :**
**Gin House Blues, Bend Me Shape Me, High In The Sky, Hello Suzie.**

**THE FOUNDATIONS**
who scored one top ten hit each year between 1967 and 1969.
Their 1969 winner was *In The Bad Bad Old Days*.

STEVIE WONDER
visited the north east in 1969 just prior
the release of his major chart hit *My Cherie Amor*

FREE at Peterlee Jazz Club prior to mega stardom.

HERMAN'S HERMITS'
ninth and penultimate top ten chart hit came in 1969 with
*My Sentimental Friend*.

## SANDIE SHAW

Sandie Shaw was born Sandra Goodrich on 26th February 1947 in Dagenham, Essex. One of the most distinctive female vocalists of the decade, she will be forever immortalised in the annals of pop history as the singer who sang barefoot on stage. Shaw's introduction to show business came after she talked her way backstage at an Adam Faith concert and met the artist's manager Eve Taylor who later signed her to a management contract and a recording deal with Pye Records. After her debut single failed to sell, she recorded a cover version of Lou Johnson's *(There's) Always Something There To Remind Me* and the Bacharach-David song topped the charts within four weeks of release in 1964. This success triggered a run of chart hits following her pairing with songwriter Chris Andrews, another of Eve Taylor's proteges who also had successes as a recording star most notably with *Yesterday Man*. In 1965, Sandie Shaw enjoyed the most successful year of her career with four chart singles including her second chart topper (the calypso styled *Long Live Love*), a top five selling LP and a successful U.K. tour with Adam Faith. By the following year her star was in the descendancy with only one top ten hit and a string of moderately selling releases, due partly to the fact that she was concentrating her promotional efforts abroad. A major U.K. comeback was successfully staged in March 1967 when Sandie was chosen to represent the U.K. in the Eurovision Song Contest with the song *Puppet On A String*. Her performance of the song gave the U.K. a first ever victory and her recording of the song reached number one on the chart in this country as well as becoming an international hit with sales in excess of four million. The success opened up new European territories to Sandie Shaw as a live performer but despite this she subsequently described the Eurovision experience in nothing but derogatory terms. With only three minor hits from the pen of Chris Andrews over the next two years, she finally had one last successful stab at the top ten in February 1969 with the Anglo/French *Monsieur Dupont* before slipping out of the limelight until sporadic returns during the mid to late eighties.

**BIGGEST 1969 HIT : Monsieur Dupont.**

**OTHER 60's CHART HITS INCLUDED :**
*(There's) Always Something There To Remind Me, Girl Don't Come,*
*I'll Stop At Nothing, Long Live Love, Message Understood,*
*Tomorrow, Puppet On A String.*

## Wearside Top Ten ~ 16th April 1969

1. I Heard It Through The Grapevine ............................................ Marvin Gaye (Tamla Motown)
2. Boom Bang-A-Bang .................................................. Lulu (Columbia)
3. Goodbye ................................................ Mary Hopkin (Apple)
4. The Israelites ........ Desmond Dekker & The Aces (Pyramid)
5. Sorry Suzanne ........................................ The Hollies (Parlophone)
6. Pinball Wizard ........................................ The Who (Track)
7. I Can Hear Music ........................................ The Beach Boys (Capitol)
8. Gentle On My Mind ........................................ Dean Martin (Reprise)
9. In The Bad Bad Old Days ................ The Foundations (Pye)
10. Games People Play ................................ Joe South (Capitol)

## Wearside Top Ten ~ 9th July 1969

1. Something In The Air ............. Thunderclap Newman (Track)
2. In The Ghetto ....................................... Elvis Presley (RCA)
3. Living In The Past ................................... Jethro Tull (Island)
4. The Ballad Of John And Yoko ............... The Beatles (Apple)
5. Break Away ................................... The Beach Boys (Capitol)
6. Hello Suzie ................................... Amen Corner (Immediate)
7. Proud Mary ............ Creedence Clearwater Revival (Liberty)
8. Way Of Life .................................... Family Dogg (Bell)
9. Oh Happy Day ................ Edwin Hawkins Singers (Buddah)
10. Frozen Orange Juice ............ Peter Sarstedt (United Artists)

# MARVIN GAYE

Despite being regarded as one of the music industry's all-time greats and a leading Motown ambassador, Marvin Gaye was not a prolific British hit maker. During the sixties, he made the charts on four occasions; twice as a soloist and once apiece with Tammi Terrell and Kim Weston. Gaye was born in Washington DC in 1939 and signed to Motown in 1961. He was an immediate recording success in his native America but in Britain his early recordings were largely ignored despite receiving great critical acclaim. Two of his earlier U.S. successes *Can I Get A Witness* and *How Sweet It Is To Be Loved By You* were subsequently popularised in this country by The Rolling Stones and Junior Walker & The All Stars respectively but it was not until 1967 that Gaye achieved the breakthrough as a recording artist. In America, Motown successfully created a 'ladies man' image for Marvin Gaye and during the mid period of the decade his dueting with a number of Motown females (Mary Wells, Kim Weston and Tammi Terrell) took precedence over his solo work. The 1967 chart debut was his duet with Weston on *It Takes Two* but he had to wait a further two years before finally cracking the U.K. chart as a solo artist. It was then a case of feast or famine as the long-awaited hit was *I Heard It Through The Grapevine* which stormed to top position and became one of the biggest selling singles of 1969. There were two further hits that year, one solo and one a duet with Tammi Terrell but the sixties were far less productive for Marvin Gaye in Britain then they were in America.

**BIGGEST 1969 HIT : I Heard It Through The Grapevine.**

**OTHER 60's CHART HITS INCLUDED :**
**Too Busy Thinking 'Bout My Baby, It Takes Two (with Kim Weston), The Onion Song (with Tammi Terrell).**

## Wearside Top Ten ~ 13th September 1969

1. In The Year 2525 ................................ Zager & Evans (RCA)
2. Bad Moon Rising .... Creedence Clearwater Revival (Liberty)
3. My Cherie Amour ............... Stevie Wonder (Tamla Motown)
4. Honky Tonk Women .................... The Rolling Stones (Decca)
5. Don't Forget To Remember .............. The Bee Gees (Polydor)
6. Too Busy Thinking 'Bout My Baby ........................................ Marvin Gaye (Tamla Motown)
7. Je T'Aime --- Moi Non Plus ........................................ Jane Birkin & Serge Gainsbourg (Major Minor)
8. Viva Bobby Joe ................................. The Equals (President)
9. Make Me An Island ..................................... Joe Dolan (Pye)
10. Saved By The Bell ............................. Robin Gibb (Polydor)

## Wearside Top Ten ~ 29th November 1969

1. Sugar Sugar .............................................. The Archies (RCA)
2. (Call Me) Number One ....................... The Tremeloes (CBS)
3. Something/Come Together ............ The Beatles (Parlophone)
4. Return Of Django ............................ The Upsetters (Upsetter)
5. Oh Well ........................................... Fleetwood Mac (Reprise)
6. Ruby Don't Take Your Love To Town ....................................... Kenny Rogers & The First Edition (Reprise)
7. Yester-Me Yester-You Yesterday ....................................... Stevie Wonder (Tamla Motown)
8. Wonderful World Beautiful People ....... Jimmy Cliff (Trojan)
9. He Ain't Heavy He's My Brother .... The Hollies (Parlophone)
10. Melting Pot ............................................. Blue Mink (Philips)

*Without Love* by Tom Jones was released and became the tenth top ten hit for the singing Welshman.

Fleetwood Mac hit top spot with *Albatross*.

Despite being closely associated with the Sixties, Martha Reeves & The Vandellas' only top ten record was the re-issue of *Dancing In The Street*. First time around in 1964 it stalled at number twenty eight.

*Wet Dream* by Max Romeo was banned by the BBC but still made the top ten.

Peter Sarstedt (brother of Eden Kane) hit the jackpot twice with the chart topping *Where Do You Go To My Lovely* and the top tenner *Frozen Orange Juice*.

After eight minor hits spanning four years, The Temptations finally made it into the top ten with *Get Ready*.

It was Vanity Fare's best year with two chart hits; *Early In The Morning* and *Hitchin' A Ride*.

**GLEN CAMPBELL**
who made his U.K. chart debut in 1969 with *Wichita Lineman.*

## TOMMY ROE

The Buddy Holly influenced boy from Georgia first shot to prominence simultaneously in Britain and America during the late summer of 1962 when the self-penned *Sheila* soared up the charts. He visited Britain the following year when he co-headlined with Chris Montez on an extensive British tour which included The Beatles as one of the supporting acts. The tour, together with numerous television and radio guest spots, kept Tommy Roe firmly in the public eye throughout 1963 and his name featured twice on the charts that year. His enrolment into the U.S. Army during 1964 removed him from the limelight and from the charts for two years; his records failing to make any impact in the absence of any personal appearances to promote their release. In 1966, Roe scored his third million seller with *Sweet Pea* which was a substantial U.S. hit and written in the so called 'bubblegum' style which became popular in both the U.S. and U.K. some two years later. His name remained in vogue in his native America during 1967/1968 during which time there was no shortage of hits but over here the name remained passé as he struggled to compete with the changing musical trends. In 1969 he was teamed with record producer Steve Barri in a career move designed to re-create his earlier Buddy Holly sound. Instead, the collaboration produced an experimental recording of a song which had been written by Tommy and long-standing friend Freddy Weller during the previous year. The song was *Dizzy* and the Barri produced recording catapulted to number one on both sides of the Atlantic selling over four million copies in the process to become Tommy Roe's biggest selling hit. The next single, *Heather Honey,* proved to be his swansong as far as the U.K. charts were concerned although he rounded off the decade with his fifth million seller, mainly on the strength of U.S. sales with *Jam Up Jelly Tight*.

*BIGGEST 1969 HIT : Dizzy.*

*OTHER 60's CHART HITS INCLUDED :*
*Sheila, Susie Darlin', The Folk Singer, Everybody, Heather Honey.*

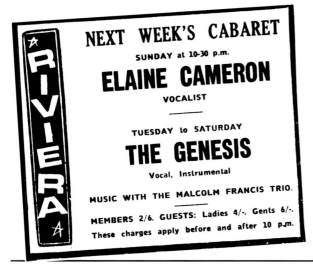
*LEFT*
**THE GENESIS**
as they were incorrectly billed in this November 1969 advertisement visited Hartlepool during their early days as a professional outfit, having played their first paid gig in September 1969 for £25.

*RIGHT*
*Sorry Suzanne* was high on the charts when **THE HOLLIES** appeared in cabaret at this Middlesbrough cabaret club.

The line up of acts booked to appear at Sunderland's various night spots in 1969 read like a who's who of showbiz. Acts appearing in the town that year included the following; many of whom progressed to be some of the biggest names of the seventies and beyond.

| DATE | ACT | VENUE |
|---|---|---|
| 5th-12th January | Don Partridge | Wetherells |
| 8th January | Family | Fillmore/Bay Hotel |
| 10th January | Simon Dupree & The Big Sound | Annabel |
| 17th January | Amen Corner | Locarno |
| 20th-26th January | Solomon King | La Strada |
| 28th January | Barry Ryan | Top Rank Suite |
| 31st January | Geno Washington/Cupid's Inspiration | Locarno |
| 3rd February | The Foundations | Annabel |
| 3rd-10th February | Dave Berry & The Cruisers | La Strada |
| 3rd February | The Pretty Things | Fillmore/Bay Hotel |
| 5th February | Johnny Johnson & The Bandwagon | Bay Hotel |
| 10th-16th February | Karl Denver Trio | La Strada |
| 14th February | The Coasters | Annabel |
| 17th February | The Herd | Annabel |
| 17th February | Pink Floyd | Fillmore/Bay Hotel |
| 17th-23rd February | The Fortunes | Wetherells |
| 17th-23rd February | Acker Bilk | La Strada |
| 21st February | Love Affair | Locarno |
| 3rd March | John Peel/Black Sabbath/Van Der Graaf Generator | Fillmore/Bay Hotel |
| 7th March | The Genesis (Note 'The' in the billing) | Club Ro-Koko |
| 7th March | Desmond Decker & The Aces | Annabel |
| 21st March | Crazy World Of Arthur Brown | Locarno |
| 24th March | Amen Corner | Top Rank Suite |
| 28th March | Cliff Bennett & The Rebel Rousers | Fillmore/Bay Hotel |
| 8th April | The Who | Fillmore/Bay Hotel |
| 9th May | Mary Wells | Annabel |
| 12th-18th May | Bobby Vee | Wetherells |
| 12th May | Chicken Shack | Fillmore/Bay Hotel |
| 16th May | Fleetwood Mac | Locarno |
| 19th May | Steppenwolf | Fillmore/Bay Hotel |
| 26th May-1st June | Kiki Dee | Wetherells |
| 26th May-1st June | Roger Whittaker | La Strada |
| 6th June | The Casuals/The Foundations | Locarno |
| 9th-15th June | Mud | Wetherells |
| 9th June | Three Dog Night | Fillmore/Bay Hotel |
| 13th June | Jethro Tull | Fillmore/Bay Hotel |
| 16th June | The Nice | Fillmore/Bay Hotel |
| 19th June | Sam The Sham | Annabel |
| 20th June | Jimmy James & The Vagabonds | Bay Hotel |
| 23rd June | Johnny Johnson & The Bandwagon | Annabel |
| 27th June | Tyrannosaurus Rex | Fillmore/Bay Hotel |
| 30th June | Yes | Fillmore/Bay Hotel |
| 30th June-6th July | Long John Baldry | Wetherells |
| 3rd July | The Equals | Locarno |
| 6th-12th July | The Caravelles | La Strada |
| 6th July | Chicken Shack | Fillmore/Bay Hotel |
| 8th July | The Tremeloes | Top Rank Suite |
| 11th July | Family | Fillmore/Bay Hotel |
| 14th July | The Crystals | Locarno |
| 15th - 26th July | Bill Hayley & His Comets | Annabel |
| 17th July | The Move | Wetherells |
| 18th July | The Who | Fillmore/Locarno |
| 4th-10th August | Carol Deene | La Strada |
| 8th August | Ambrose Slade | Annabel |
| 17th-23rd August | Love Affair | Wetherells |
| 22nd August | Family | Fillmore/Locarno |
| 1st August - 6th September | Dave Dee, Dozy, Beaky, Mick & Tich | Wetherells |
| 1st September | 5th Dimension | Manhattan |
| 8th-11th September | The Fourmost | Wetherells |
| 12th September | Free/Mott The Hoople | Fillmore/Locarno |
| 22nd September | The Casuals | Wetherells |
| 4th October | The Pretty Things | Bay Hotel |
| 17th October | Family | Fillmore/Locarno |
| 19th-25th October | The Grumbleweeds | La Strada |
| 21st October | The Troggs | Top Rank Suite |
| 24th October | John Peel/Pink Floyd | Fillmore/Locarno |
| 24th October | Slade (Note 'Ambrose' has been dropped from name) | Annabel |
| 27th October | Lovin' Spoonful | Annabel |
| 30th October | The Move | Top Rank Suite |
| 1st November | Sandie Shaw/The Troggs | Sunderland Empire |

| | | |
|---|---|---|
| 4th November | Marv Johnson | Top Rank Suite |
| 8th November | The Casuals | Annabel |
| 10th November | The Pretty Things | Annabel |
| 18th November | Love Affair | Annabel |
| 21st November | 1910 Fruitgum Company | Annabel |
| 28th November | Tyrannosaurus Rex | Fillmore/Locarno |
| 5th December | Marv Johnson | Annabel |
| 5th December | The Pretty Things | Seaburn Hall |
| 14th-20th December | The Searchers | La Strada |
| 16th December | Lou Christie | Top Rank Suite |
| 18th December | The Drifters | Bay Hotel |

The Fillmore Organisation ceased its promotional activities at Bay Hotel on 21st July after which time it was represented at the Locarno Ballroom.

The Manhattan was the re-named Porama Club which had closed during the year.

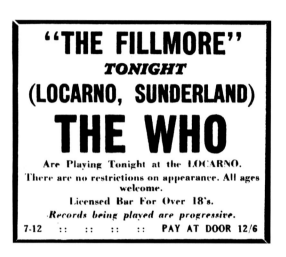

LEFT
The Fillmore Organisation staged shows on Wearside at The Bay Hotel and The Barnes Hotel before moving to the larger Locarno Ballroom where they promoted this show with THE WHO in 1969.

RIGHT
*See Emily Play* hit the top ten in 1967 and two years later the creators of the song were at the Bay Hotel where you could see them for 7/6.

## The Ones That Got Away In ...

1969

| | |
|---|---|
| *Plastic Man* | The Kinks |
| *You've Made Me So Very Happy* | Blood, Sweat & Tears |
| *She Sold Me Magic* | Lou Christie |
| *Are You Growing Tired Of My Love* | Status Quo |
| *Breakfast On Pluto* | Don Partridge |
| *Everybody's Talkin'* | Nilsson |
| *Tragedy* | Brian Hyland |

*Plastic Man* became only the second Kinks' single to miss the top twenty since the group's chart debut in 1964. The main reason for its failure was a BBC airplay ban resulting from the inclusion of the word 'bum' in the song's lyrics.

Status Quo suffered a chart set back relatively early in their career. Prior to their eventual 12 bar blues sound the group experimented with psychedelia, ballads and straight pop. *Are You Growing Tired Of My Love* was a beat ballad which was all but totally rejected by the fans and was a musical direction which the group quickly abandoned.

American rock group Blood, Sweat & Tears scored a massive hit in their homeland with *You've Made Me So Very Happy*. Over here, the record missed the top thirty entirely and was probably released a year or so too soon for British tastes. Twelve months on and the likes of Black Sabbath and Deep Purple were registering chart hits with commercial rock singles at which point *You've Made Me So Very Happy* which surely have reaped its just rewards.

# QUIZ QUESTIONS

## Part A

1. NAME THE FIRST TOP TEN HITS BY THE FOLLOWING ACTS:-
   (a) Billy J. Kramer & The Dakotas
   (b) Manfred Mann
   (c) The Move
   (d) Creedence Clearwater Revival
   (e) The Seekers
   (f) Del Shannon

2. WHICH CHART NAMES EXPERIENCED THEIR FINAL MOMENT OF CHART GLORY WITH THE FOLLOWING NUMBERS:-
   (a) 'Boys Cry'
   (b) 'Bobby Tomorrow'
   (c) 'Applejack'
   (d) 'Too Many Rivers'
   (e) 'Pamela Pamela'
   (f) 'Snake In The Grass'

3. THE FOLLOWING SONGS WERE SOLO HITS FOR FORMER OR CURRENT MEMBERS OF CHART GROUPS AT THAT TIME. NAME THEM:-
   (a) 'Death Of A Clown'
   (b) 'High Time'
   (c) 'San Franciscan Nights'
   (d) 'Come On Home'
   (e) 'Just Like Eddie'
   (f) 'Joanna'

4. WHAT ARE THE STAGE NAMES OF THE FOLLOWING PEOPLE:-
   (a) Ronald Wycherley
   (b) Concetta Franconero
   (c) Robert Zimmerman
   (d) Terry Perkins
   (e) Carole Klein
   (f) Frank Castelluccio

5. THE FOLLOWING SONGS WERE WELL KNOWN 'B' SIDES OF SIXTIES HITS. NAME THE 'A' SIDES:-
   (a) 'Kelly' (Del Shannon)
   (b) 'Mean Woman Blues' (Roy Orbison)
   (c) 'Strawberry Fields Forever' (The Beatles)
   (d) 'So Sad' (The Everly Brothers)
   (e) 'The Stranger' (The Shadows)
   (f) 'Who Am I' (Adam Faith)

6. NAME THE FIRST NUMBER ONE HIT BY THE FOLLOWING ACTS:-
   (a) The Beatles
   (b) Roy Orbison
   (c) Helen Shapiro
   (d) The Rolling Stones
   (e) The Beach Boys
   (f) The Shadows

7. THE FOLLOWING SONGS WERE ALL COVER VERSION HITS BUT WHO HAD THE ORIGINAL AMERICAN HIT WITH THE SONGS:-
   (a)  'Tell Him' (Billie Davis)
   (b)  'Anyone Who Had A Heart' (Cilla Black)
   (c)  'When My Little Girl Is Smiling' (Craig Douglas and Jimmy Justice)
   (d)  'Cupid' (Johnny Nash)
   (e)  'Message To Martha' (Adam Faith)
   (f)  'Bend Me Shape Me' (Amen Corner)

8. THE FOLLOWING ACTS ALL HAD A TOP TEN HIT WITH A COLOUR IN THE TITLE. NAME THE SONGS:-
   (a)  Don Partridge
   (b)  Los Bravos
   (c)  Tom Jones
   (d)  The Marcels
   (e)  The Scaffold
   (f)  Jacky

9. WHO HAD SEASONAL SOUNDING HITS WITH THE FOLLOWING SONGS:-
   (a)  'Winter World Of Love'
   (b)  'Summer In The City'
   (c)  'Summer Nights'
   (d)  'Autumn Almanac'
   (e)  'In Summer'
   (f)  'Theme From A Summer Place'

10. EACH OF THE FOLLOWING ACTS HAD A TOP TEN HIT WITH A PLACE NAME IN THE TITLE. NAME THE SONG:-
   (a)  The Bee Gees
   (b)  Gene Pitney
   (c)  The Kinks
   (d)  Tom Jones
   (e)  New Vaudeville Band
   (f)  Kenny Ball & His Jazzmen

11. NAME THE SINGERS WITH THE FOLLOWING BACKING GROUPS:-
   (a)  The Roulettes
   (b)  The Bruvvers
   (c)  The Fenmen
   (d)  The Pirates
   (e)  The Blue Flames
   (f)  The Union Gap

12. NAME THE RECOGNISED LEAD SINGERS OF THE FOLLOWING GROUPS:-
   (a)  The Hollies
   (b)  The Kinks
   (c)  The Four Seasons
   (d)  Manfred Mann (1964-1966)
   (e)  Manfred Mann (1966-1969)
   (f)  The Troggs

13. WHICH GROUPS INCLUDED THE FOLLOWING LEAD SINGERS IN THEIR LINE-UP:-
   (a)  Andy Fairweather-Low
   (b)  Denny Laine
   (c)  Davy Jones
   (d)  Dean Ford
   (e)  Levi Stubbs
   (f)  Stevie Winwood

4. ON WHICH RECORD LABEL DID THE FOLLOWING ACTS SCORE THEIR CHART HITS IN THE SIXTIES:-
   (a) Billy Fury
   (b) Gerry & The Pacemakers
   (c) The Searchers
   (d) Brenda Lee
   (e) The Bee Gees
   (f) Neil Sedaka

5. WHICH FAMOUS RECORDING STARS WROTE OR CO-WROTE THE FOLLOWING CHART HITS:-
   (a) 'That Girl Belongs To Yesterday' (Gene Pitney)
   (b) 'Build Me Up Buttercup' (The Foundations)
   (c) 'Swiss Maid' (Del Shannon)
   (d) 'Where The Boys Are' (Connie Francis)
   (e) 'Michelle' (The Overlanders)
   (f) 'Hello Mary Lou' (Ricky Nelson)

6. THE ACTS WHO RECORDED THE FOLLOWING SONGS ALL MADE IT TO NUMBER ONE BUT SUBSEQUENTLY BECAME 'ONE HIT WONDERS'. NAME THE ACTS:-
   (a) 'Tell Laura I Love Her'
   (b) 'In The Year 2525'
   (c) 'Nut Rocker'
   (d) 'Fire'
   (e) 'Sugar Sugar'
   (f) 'Michelle'

7. NAME THE YEAR IN WHICH:-
   (a) 'Love Me Do' gave the Beatles their first hit.
   (b) 'Crying In The Chapel' became Elvis Presley's last number one of the decade.
   (c) 'Telstar' was a massive transatlantic hit for The Tornados.
   (d) Frank Sinatra topped the charts with 'Strangers In The Night'.
   (e) Sandie Shaw's 'Puppet On A String' won the Eurovision Song Contest.
   (f) Thunderclap Newman scored a solitary sixties hit with the chart topping 'Something In The Air'.

8. NUMBERS OFTEN CROPPED UP IN SIXTIES SONG TITLES.
   EACH OF THESE ACTS HAD ONE TOP TEN HIT WHICH CONTAINED A NUMBER OR NUMBERS IN THE TITLE. NAME THE SONGS:-
   (a) Connie Stevens
   (b) Johnny Burnette
   (c) Len Barry
   (d) The Dubliners
   (e) Rolf Harris
   (f) Bobby Vee

9. THE FOLLOWING ACTS ALL SCORED A HIT WITH A REFERENCE TO ROYALTY IN THE TITLE. NAME THE SONGS:-
   (a) Helen Shapiro
   (b) Neil Sedaka
   (c) Ned Miller
   (d) Gene Pitney
   (e) Roger Miller
   (f) The Hollies

20. THE FOLLOWING ACTS ALL SCORED A HIT WITH WEATHER IN THE TITLE. NAME THE SONGS:-
    (a)   The Kinks
    (b)   Jimi Hendrix
    (c)   Herman's Hermits
    (d)   The Cascades
    (e)   Bob Dylan
    (f)   The Walker Brothers

21. THE FOLLOWING ACTS ALL SCORED A HIT WITH A MALE NAME IN THE TITLE. NAME THE SONGS:-
    (a)   Twinkle
    (b)   Cat Stevens
    (c)   Bernard Cribbins
    (d)   John Leyton
    (e)   Tho Who
    (f)   1910 Fruitgum Co.

22. THE FOLLOWING ACTS ALL SCORED A HIT WITH A FEMALE NAME IN THE TITLE. NAME THE SONGS:-
    (a)   The Who
    (b)   Brian Hyland
    (c)   Marv Johnson
    (d)   The Four Pennies
    (e)   Nat King Cole
    (f)   Joe Brown

23. THE WORD 'BABY' WAS PREVALENT IN SIXTIES SONGS. EACH OF THE FOLLOWING ACTS HAD ONE HIT WITH 'BABY' IN THE TITLE. NAME THE SONGS:-
    (a)   The Equals
    (b)   Sonny & Cher
    (c)   The Foundations
    (d)   Bruce Channel
    (e)   Them
    (f)   The Supremes

24. FOOD IS AN UNUSUAL TOPIC TO USE IN A RECORD TITLE. THE FOLLOWING ACTS ALL HAD A CHART HIT WHICH CONTAINED A WORD IN THE TITLE WHICH RELATED TO A FOOD SUBSTANCE. NAME THE RECORDS:-
    (a)   The Newbeats
    (b)   Little Eva
    (c)   Bobby Goldsboro
    (d)   Nancy Sinatra
    (e)   Tornados
    (f)   Johnny & The Hurricanes

25. SEVEN OF THE DECADE'S CHART TOPPERS INCLUDED A BRACKET IN THE TITLE. IDENTIFY THE WORDS IN THE EMPTY BRACKETS:-
    (a)   '(_ _ _ _ _   _ _ _) Devil In Disguise'
    (b)   'San Francisco (_ _   _ _ _ _   _ _   _ _ _ _   _ _ _   _ _ _ _ _ _ _   _ _   _ _ _ _   _ _ _ _
    (c)   '(_   _ _ _ _   _ _ _   _ _) Satisfaction'
    (d)   '(_ _ _ _ _ _) Always Something There To Remind Me'
    (e)   '(_ _   _ _ _ _ _ _ _ _ _   _ _) Half As Nice'
    (f)   'Where Are You Now (_ _   _ _ _ _)'
    (g)   'In The Years 2525 (_ _ _ _ _ _ _   _ _ _   _ _ _ _ _ _ _)'

26. SIX OF THE MANY CHART HITS TO USE THE WORD 'GIRL' IN THE TITLE ARE LISTED BELOW. NAME THE ACT WHO HAD A HIT WITH THE SONG:-
   (a) 'With A Girl Like You'
   (b) 'Hello Little Girl'
   (c) 'Girl Don't Come'
   (d) 'Shy Girl'
   (e) 'Hey Little Girl'
   (f) 'The Girl Who Sang The Blues'

27. BACHARACH-DAVID WERE TWO OF THE MOST PROLIFIC SONGWRITERS OF THE SIXTIES. SIX OF THEIR HITS ARE LISTED BELOW. WHO SCORED HITS IN THE BRITISH CHARTS WITH THE SONGS:-
   (a) 'Walk On By'
   (b) 'I Just Don't Know What To Do With Myself'
   (c) 'Alfie'
   (d) 'I Say A Little Prayer'
   (e) 'I'll Never Fall In Love Again'
   (f) 'Make It Easy On Yourself'

28. SIX NATIONALITIES ARE REPRESENTED BY THE HIT SINGLES LISTED BELOW. NAME THE ACT AND THE COUNTRY REPRESENTED:-
   (a) 'Dominique'
   (b) 'Cinderella Rockefella'
   (c) 'Sukiyaki' (original recording)
   (d) 'Sun Arise'
   (e) 'If I Only Had Time'
   (f) 'If I Loved You'

29. THE FOLLOWING ACTS EACH HAD A HIT SINGLE WHICH CONTAINED A REFERENCE TO A MODE OF TRANSPORT IN THE TITLE. NAME THE SONGS:-
   (a) The Hollies
   (b) Lulu
   (c) The Walker Brothers
   (d) Reparata & The Delrons
   (e) Herb Alpert
   (f) Billy J. Kramer & The Dakotas
   (g) Cliff Richard

30. THERE WERE ONLY SIX HIT SINGLES DURING THE ENTIRE DECADE TO CONTAIN THE WORD 'CHRISTMAS' IN THE TITLE. NAME THE SONGS:-

31. FIVE OF THE BEATLES' CHART HITS CONTAINED A GIRL'S NAME IN THE 'A' SIDE TITLE. NAME THE SONGS:-

32. WHO HAD SIXTIES TOP TEN HITS WITH THE FOLLOWING INSTRUMENTALS:-
   (a) 'Nut Rocker'
   (b) 'Theme From Z Cars'
   (c) 'Wipe Out'
   (d) 'Cast Your Fate To The Wind'
   (e) 'Maria Elena'
   (f) 'The Good The Bad And The Ugly'

33. ONLY THREE PEOPLE WITH THE NAME 'SMITH' HAD A TOP TWENTY HIT THROUGHOUT THE SIXTIES. NAME THE PEOPLE AND THE SONGS:-

34. THE FOLLOWING ACTS ALL HAD A TOP TEN HIT WITH THE NAME OF A MUSICAL INSTRUMENT IN THE TITLE. NAME THE SONGS:-
   (a) Duane Eddy
   (b) Ken Dodd
   (c) Sandy Nelson
   (d) The Shadows

# Part B

1. Who had a top three hit with *Are You Sure* and represented the U.K. with the song in the 1961 Eurovision Song Contest.

2. Eric Burdon and Alan Price were members of which sixties pop group.

3. Who dropped the letter 'y' from his christian name in 1961 and successfully revived the thirties classic *For You* in 1964.

4. Name Joe South's solitary sixties hit.

5. Who left Durham Town in 1969.

6. What was the title of Louis Armstrong's only sixties chart topper.

7. Who had a hit with *Mockingbird Hill* in 1964.

8. Colin Blunstone and Rod Argent were founder members of this group which experienced greater successes in the US than on home soil. Name the group.

9. Decca launched a trendy new record label in 1966. Name it.

10. Who sang lead vocals on The Supremes' first U.K. chart hit *Where Did Our Love Go*.

11. Which sugar sweet American couple hit the charts twice in rapid succession during 1963 with *Hey Paula* and *Young Lovers*.

12. Name Pink Floyd's only top ten hit in the sixties.

13. Which was the first Beatles album to be released on the Apple label.

14. Peter Frampton fronted two sixties chart groups. Name them.

15. With whom did Bobbie Gentry duet on the 1969 hit *All I Have To Do Is Dream*.

16. Which Shakespeare title did Adam Faith take into the 1962 charts.

17. Whose first ever chart hit was *Space Oddity*.

18. In which year did Cupid's Inspiration chart with *Yesterday Has Gone*.

19. Two acts charted simultaneously with *All I Really Want To Do* in 1965. Name them.

20. What was the title of The Bonzo Dog Doo-Dah Band's only chart hit.

21. Which year was the so-called 'Summer Of Love'.

22. *Toy* was the follow up to which 1968 chart hit.

23. Chris Andrews wrote several hits for Sandie Shaw and Adam Faith. With which song did he make his chart debut as a singer in 1965.

24. Whose only U.K. top ten hit was *If I Had A Hammer*.

25. What was Simon & Garfunkel's first U.K. top ten hit.

26. Name Lonnie Donegan's only number one of the sixties.

27. Which radio station could be found on 208 frequency on the medium wave band.

28. In which year did Shirley Ellis crack the top ten with *The Clapping Song*.

29. Which fairground attraction did The Everly Brothers sing about in 1964.

30. Whose tenth and final top ten hit was *Vacation*.

31. Gerry Dorsey found fame and fortune with eight top ten hits between 1967 and 1969. Under which name were the recordings made.

32. The Beach Boys topped the U.K. charts twice during the sixties. The first time was with *Good Vibrations* in 1966 and then again in 1968 with which song.

33. On which record label did Bob Dylan have six top ten hits in the sixties.

34. Simon Dupree & The Big Sound had just one top ten hit. Name it.

35. Which Columbia recording act had a number one hit in each of 1964, 1966 and 1967 but no further top ten hits during the entire decade.

36. A group with strong local connections enjoyed their one moment of chart glory in 1968 when *Everything I Am*, achieved top ten status. Name the group.

37. Which of Jim Reeves' records was climbing the charts at the time of his death.

38. In which year did Alan Price first hit the charts after leaving The Animals. The song concerned was *I Put A Spell On You*.

39. Who made her barefooted chart debut on 1964.

40. Who was the resident host of the BBC Light Programme's Saturday Club.

41. Which comedian had a 1963 top twenty hit with *Harvest Of Love*.

42. Who charted with the classic 1969 recording of *Oh Happy Day*.

43. Who had a fall out with his brothers and was *Saved By The Bell* in 1969.

44. The Jonathan King inspired hit *It's Good News Week* was a 1965 hit for a group of RAF servicemen. Which name did King give the group.

45. Brian Poole's former backing group had a string of hits from 1967 onwards after splitting from Poole and establishing themselves as a recording outfit in their own right. Name the group.

46. Which group mixed *Concrete And Clay*.

47. Cliff Bennett & The Rebel Rousers successfully covered *Got To Get You Into My Life* in 1966. On which Beatles' LP was the song to be found.

48. Ian Anderson was lead singer with which sixties chart group.

49. Whose first hit was *Funny How Love Can Be*.

50. In which year did The Monkees first hit the U.K. charts.

51. Peter Noone was lead singer with which sixties chart group.

52. They hitched a ride and lived for the sun early in the morning. Who were they.

53. Who had a 'one-off' hit in 1966 with *Supergirl*.

54. What was the original title of Manfred Mann's *Semi-Detached Suburban Mr. James* and why was it changed.

55. A spin-off duo from The Merseybeats had a hit in 1966 with *Sorrow*. Name the duo.

56. Name the first record to be played on Radio One.

57. *Sweet William* was a similar sounding follow-up to which top three hit.

58. Four of The Troggs' five top ten hits were released in the same year. Which one.

59. Eric Clapton, Jeff Beck and Jimmy Page were members of this group at various times during the mid sixties. Name the group.

60. Which subsequent chart star of the eighties played lead guitar on The Equals' 1968 number one hit *Baby Come Back*.

61. The Fourmost's first two hits were written by Lennon & McCartney. The first one was *Hello Little Girl* but what was the second.

62. Val Doonican had a 1965 hit with a cover version of an American song. Both his version and the original peaked at number five. Name the song and the American singer/songwriter who enjoyed equal success with Doonican in this country.

63. Between August 1963 and November 1964 only one American act topped the British charts and managed to do it with two songs. Name the act and the songs.

64. Nina & Frederick had just one U.K. top ten hit. The song was *Little Donkey* but what was the year.

65. Who sang *Walk Right In* in 1963.

66. Bobby Elliott was drummer with which sixties chart group.

67. Barry McGuire predicted doom and gloom in 1965 with which song.

68. *Twist And Shout* was a 1963 chart hit for both The Beatles and Brian Poole & The Tremeloes but who first popularised the song in Britain earlier that year.

69. Who scored a major hit in 1967 with *It Must Be Him*.

70. Which fifties/early sixties recording star saw her chart career reactivated by songwriter and producer Tony Hatch during the mid sixties.

71. Tina Turner's top ten debut was with *River Deep Mountain High* in 1966. Her instrumentalist husband shared the record label credits with her. Name him.

72. Two acts successfully covered Lennon & McCartney's *Michelle*. The Overlanders were one but name the other.

73. Jimmy Saville hosted the TTDC on Radio Luxembourg during the early to mid sixties. What did the letters stand for.

74. In the early sixties the charts were dominated by the major record companies EMI, Decca, Pye, Philips and their associated labels. However, in 1962 Maureen Evans flew the flag of the independent record companies when she soared into the top ten. Name the song and the label.

75. Which fellow Decca recording artiste and Andrew Loog Oldham - managed act hit the charts with the Mick Jagger/Keith Richard song *As Tears Go By* for a chart debut in 1964.

76. Who hosted the television pop music show Discs A Go-Go.

77. In 1964, which 'word' was used six times on a top five song title.

78. Who sang *Fanlight Fanny* in 1962 and *Run To The Door* in 1967.

79. Who revived Tennessee Ernie Ford's fifties chart topper *Give Me Your Word* and in doing so scored his final top thirty hit of the decade.

80. Which Coronation Street actor had a surprise 1964 hit with *Not Too Little Not Too Much*.

81. Which duo utilised the songwriting talents of Paul McCartney (twice), Buddy Holly & Phil Spector for their first four U.K. top ten hits.

82. In 1968, who won a heat of Opportunity Knocks, was signed by Paul McCartney to the Apple record label and scored a number one hit with her first single release.

83. During the sixties, countless American hits were released in Britain under licence by the Decca Record Company on which of its associated labels.

84. Peter Sarstedt was a late sixties hit recording artist while his brother Richard hit the charts earlier in the decade. Under which name was Richard Sarstedt better known.

85. In which year was Jonathan King first unleashed upon an unsuspecting British public with the release of *Everyone's Gone To The Moon*.

86. What was the domestic connection between the composers and the singer of the 1962 hit *The Locomotion*.

87. Which group had a top ten hit in 1964 with *Everything's Alright*.

88. Bobby Rydell scored a minor Christmas hit in 1962 with Jingle Bell Rock. Which other American chart star sang on the record.

89. Which sixties group comprised Roger Daltrey, Pete Townsend, Keith Moon and John Entwhistle.

90. 'The Weekend Starts Here' were the opening words of which weekly television pop music programme.

91. Which legendary record producer issued the classic LP *A Christmas Gift For You* in 1963.

92. Which female twosome sang *You Don't Have To Be A Baby To Cry* in 1963 and then sank into chart oblivion.

93. Comedy actor Bernard Cribbins was a surprise chart climber in 1962 with two top ten hits. Name them.

94. Which group was launched as 'Tottenham's Answer To The Beatles'.

95. Cilla Black's debut single was a Lennon & McCartney composition. Name it.

96. Which group did Decca sign in 1962 in preference to The Beatles.

97. When The Hollies released a cover version of a Beatles' track in 1965, George Harrison publicly criticised the recording. It became one of the The Hollies' poorest selling singles of the sixties. What was the title.

98. Whose recording career suffered a severe downturn when he left the relatively small Monument label in America for the mighty MGM. Upon his own insistence, his releases remained on London American in Britain.

99. What was unusual about the 'B' side of *They're Coming To Take Me Away Ha-Haaa* by Napoleon IV.

100. Which sixties recording star had the same name as that of his record label.

## *Answers to Part A*

(a) 'Do You Want To Know A Secret'
(b) '5-4-3-2-1'
(c) 'Night Of Fear'
(d) 'Proud Mary'
(e) 'I'll Never Find Another You'
(f) 'Runaway'                    **(6 Points)**

(a) Eden Kane
(b) Bobby Vee
(c) Jet Harris & Tony Meehan
(d) Brenda Lee
(e) Wayne Fontana
(f) Dave Dee, Dozy, Beaky, Mick & Tich    **(6 Points)**

(a) Dave Davies
(b) Paul Jones
(c) Eric Burdon
(d) Wayne Fontana
(e) Heinz
(f) Scott Walker                 **(6 Points)**

(a) Billy Fury
(b) Connie Francis
(c) Bob Dylan
(d) Craig Douglas
(e) Carole King
(f) Frankie Valli                **(6 Points)**

(a) 'Two Kinds Of Teardrops'
(b) 'Blue Bayou'
(c) 'Penny Lane'
(d) 'Lucille'
(e) 'Man Of Mystery'
(f) 'This Is It'                  **(6 Points)**

(a) 'From Me To You'
(b) 'Only The Lonely'
(c) 'You Don't Know'
(d) 'It's All Over Now'
(e) 'Good Vibrations'
(f) 'Apache'                     **(6 Points)**

(a) The Exciters
(b) Dionne Warwick
(c) The Drifters
(d) Sam Cooke
(e) Lou Johnson
(f) The American Breed           **(6 Points)**

(a) 'Blue Eyes'
(b) 'Black Is Black'
(c) 'Green Green Grass Of Home'
(d) 'Blue Moon'
(e) 'Lily The Pink'
(f) 'White Horses'               **(6 Points)**

9. (a) Engelbert Humperdinck
   (b) Lovin' Spoonful
   (c) Marianne Faithfull
   (d) The Kinks
   (e) Billy Fury
   (f) Percy Faith               **(6 Points)**

10. (a) 'Massachusetts'
    (b) 'Twenty Four Hours From Tulsa'
    (c) 'Waterloo Sunset'
    (d) 'Detroit City'
    (e) 'Winchester Cathedral'
    (f) 'Midnight In Moscow'      **(6 Points)**

11. (a) Adam Faith
    (b) Joe Brown
    (c) Bern Elliott
    (d) Johnny Kidd
    (e) Georgie Fame
    (f) Gary Puckett             **(6 Points)**

12. (a) Allan Clarke
    (b) Ray Davies
    (c) Frankie Valli
    (d) Paul Jones
    (e) Mike D'Abo
    (f) Reg Presley              **(6 Points)**

13. (a) Amen Corner
    (b) The Moody Blues
    (c) The Monkees
    (d) Marmalade
    (e) The Four Tops
    (f) The Spencer Davis Group   **(6 Points)**

14. (a) Decca
    (b) Columbia
    (c) Pye
    (d) Brunswick
    (e) Polydor
    (f) RCA                      **(6 Points)**

15. (a) Mick Jagger & Keith Richard
    (b) Mike D'Abo
    (c) Roger Miller
    (d) Neil Sedaka
    (e) John Lennon & Paul McCartney
    (f) Gene Pitney             **(6 Points)**

16. (a) Ricky Valance
    (b) Zager & Evans
    (c) B. Bumble & The Stingers
    (d) The Crazy World Of Arthur Brown
    (e) The Archies
    (f) The Overlanders         **(6 Points)**

17. (a) 1962
    (b) 1965
    (c) 1962
    (d) 1966
    (e) 1967
    (f) 1969 *(6 Points)*

18. (a) 'Sixteen Reasons'
    (b) 'You're Sixteen'
    (c) '1-2-3'
    (d) 'Seven Drunken Nights'
    (e) 'Two Little Boys'
    (f) 'The Night Has A Thousand Eyes' *(6 Points)*

19. (a) 'Queen For Tonight'
    (b) 'King Of Clowns'
    (c) 'From A Jack To A King'
    (d) 'Princess In Rags'
    (e) 'King Of The Road'
    (f) 'King Midas In Reverse' *(6 Points)*

20. (a) 'Sunny Afternoon'
    (b) 'The Wind Cries Mary'
    (c) 'Sunshine Girl'
    (d) 'Rhythm Of The Rain'
    (e) 'Rainy Day Women Nos 12 & 35'
    (f) 'The Sun Ain't Gonna Shine Anymore' *(6 Points)*

21. (a) 'Terry'
    (b) 'Mathew And Son'
    (c) 'Right Said Fred'
    (d) 'Johnny Remember Me'
    (e) 'Happy Jack'
    (f) 'Simon Says' *(6 Points)*

22. (a) 'Pictures Of Lily'
    (b) 'Ginny Come Lately'
    (c) 'I'll Pick A Rose For My Rose'
    (d) 'Juliet'
    (e) 'Ramblin' Rose'
    (f) 'Sally Ann' *(6 Points)*

23. (a) 'Baby Come Back'
    (b) 'Baby Don't Go'
    (c) 'Baby Now That I've Found You'
    (d) 'Hey Baby'
    (e) 'Baby Please Don't Go'
    (f) 'Baby Love' *(6 Points)*

24. (a) 'Bread And Butter'
    (b) 'Let's Turkey Trot'
    (c) 'Honey'
    (d) 'Sugar Town'
    (e) 'Ice Cream Man'
    (f) 'Rocking Goose' *(6 Points)*

25. (a) (You're The)
    (b) (Be Sure To Wear Some Flowers In Your Hair)
    (c) (I Can't Get No)
    (d) (There's)
    (e) (If Paradise Is)
    (f) (My Love)
    (g) (Exordium And Terminus) *(7 Points)*

26. (a) The Troggs
    (b) The Fourmost
    (c) Sandie Shaw
    (d) Mark Wynter
    (e) Del Shannon
    (f) The Everly Brothers *(6 Points)*

27. (a) Dionne Warwick
    (b) Dusty Springfield
    (c) Cilla Black
    (d) Aretha Franklin
    (e) Bobbie Gentry
    (f) The Walker Brothers *(6 Points)*

28. (a) The Singing Nun (Belgium)
    (b) Esther & Abi Ofarim (Israel)
    (c) Kyu Sakamoto (Japan)
    (d) Rolf Harris (Australia)
    (e) John Rowles (New Zealand)
    (f) Richard Anthony (France) *(6 Points)*

29. (a) 'Bus Stop'
    (b) 'The Boat That I Row'
    (c) 'My Ship Is Coming In'
    (d) 'Captain Of Your Ship'
    (e) 'Tijuana Taxi'
    (f) 'Trains And Boats And Planes'
    (g) 'Big Ship' *(7 Points)*

30. (a) 'If Everyday Was Like Christmas'
    (b) 'Lonely Pup (In A Christmas Shop)'
    (c) 'Blue Christmas'
    (d) 'Rockin' Around The Christmas Tree'
    (e) 'Christmas Will Be Just Another Lonely Day'
    (f) 'All I Want For Christmas Is A Beatle' *(6 Points)*

31. (a) 'Eleanor Rigby'
    (b) 'Penny Lane'
    (c) 'Lady Madonna'
    (d) 'Hey Jude'
    (e) 'The Ballad of John and Yoko' *(5 Points)*

32. (a) B. Bumble & The Stingers
    (b) Johnny Keating
    (c) The Surfaris
    (d) Sounds Orchestral
    (e) Los Indios Tabajaras
    (f) Hugo Montenegro *(6 Points)*

33. (a) Keely Smith
        'You're Breakin' My Heart'
    (b) Whistling Jack Smith
        'I Was Kaiser Bill's Batman'
    (c) O.C. Smith
        'Son Of Hickory Holler's Tramp' *(3 Points)*

34. (a) '(Dance With) The Guitar Man'
    (b) 'Love Is Like A Violin'
    (c) 'Let There Be Drums'
    (d) 'Guitar Tango' *(4 Points)*

**(TOTAL 200 POINTS**

## Answers to Part B

(ONE POINT FOR EACH COMPLETE ANSWER)

. The Allisons
. The Animals
. Rick(y) Nelson
. 'The Games People Play'
. Roger Whittaker
. 'What A Wonderful World'
. The Migil Five
. The Zombies
. Deram
0. Diana Ross
1. Paul & Paula
2. 'See Emily Play'
3. The Beatles (aka The White Album)
4. The Herd and Humble Pie
5. Glen Campbell
6. 'As You Like It'
7. David Bowie
8. 1968
9. The Byrds and Cher
0. 'I'm The Urban Spaceman'
1. 1967
2. 'Jesamine' (The Casuals)
3. 'Yesterday Man'
4. Trini Lopez
5. 'Homeward Bound'
6. 'My Old Man's A Dustman'
7. Radio Luxembourg
8. 1965
9. 'The Ferris Wheel'
0. Connie Francis
1. Engelbert Humperdinck
2. 'Do It Again'
3. CBS
4. 'Kites'
5. Georgie Fame & The Blue Flames
6. Plastic Penny
7. 'I Won't Forget You'
8. 1966
9. Sandie Shaw
0. Brian Mathew
. Benny Hill
2. The Edwin Hawkins Singers
3. Robin Gibb
4. Hedgehoppers Anonymous
5. The Tremeloes
6. Unit Four Plus Two
7. 'Revolver'
8. Jethro Tull
9. The Ivy League
0. 1967
. Herman's Hermits
. Vanity Fare

53. Graham Bonney
54. 'Semi-Detached Suburban Mr. Jones'
    It was changed in case it was misinterpreted as a reference to ex lead singer Paul Jones.
55. The Merseys
56. 'Flowers In The Rain' (The Move)
57. 'My Boy Lollipop' (Millie)
58. 1966
59. The Yardbirds
60. Eddy Grant
61. 'I'm In Love'
62. 'Elusive Butterfly' (Bob Lind)
63. Roy Orbison
    'It's Over' and 'Oh Pretty Woman'
64. 1960
65. The Rooftop Singers
66. The Hollies
67. 'Eve Of Destruction'
68. The Isley Brothers
69. Vikki Carr
70. Petula Clark
71. Ike Turner
72. David & Jonathan
73. Teen & Twenty Disc Club
74. 'Like I Do' / Oriole
75. Marianne Faithfull
76. Kent Walton
77. Um
78. Clinton Ford
79. Billy Fury
80. Chris Sandford
81. Peter & Gordon
82. Mary Hopkin
83. London American
84. Eden Kane
85. 1965
86. Little Eva was Carole King's babysitter.
87. The Mojos
88. Chubby Checker
89. The Who
90. Ready Steady Go
91. Phil Spector
92. The Caravelles
93. 'Hole In The Ground' and 'Right Said Fred'
94. The Dave Clark Five
95. 'Love Of The Loved'
96. Brian Poole & The Tremeloes
97. 'If I Needed Someone'
98. Roy Orbison
99. It was the 'A' side recording in reverse
100. Wayne Fontana

**(TOTAL 100 POINTS)**